MW01675181

EXPLICIT THOUGHTS

BY SHAZARDES G. RICHARDS

FIND *EXPLICIT THOUGHTS* ON THE WEB:
Instagram Page: Explicitthoughts2020
Facebook Page: https://www.facebook.com/shazardes.richards.9
Twitter Page: Explicitthoughts
Link to my Biography
Link to my Blog
Email Address: EXPLICITTHOUGHTS2020@GMAIL.COM

Explicit Thoughts
Copyright © 2020 by Shazardes G. Richards

All rights reserved. No part of this publication may be reproduced, distributed, or transmitted in any form or by any means, including photocopying, recording, or other electronic or mechanical methods, without the prior written permission of the author, except in the case of brief quotations embodied in critical reviews and certain other non-commercial uses permitted by copyright law.

tellwell

Tellwell Talent
www.tellwell.ca

ISBN
978-0-2288-1821-2 (Hardcover)
978-0-2288-1822-9 (Paperback)
978-0-2288-1823-6 (eBook)

TABLE OF CONTENTS

EXPLICIT THOUGHTS (Introduction) v
Chapter 1: EXPLICIT THOUGHTS (Poems One to Thirteen) 1
Chapter 2: FEELINGS ABOUT A RELATIONSHIP (Poems One to Twelve) 21
Chapter 3: ANGRY (Poems One to Thirteen) 47
Chapter 4: TWISTED EXPLICIT (Poems One to Fourteen) 71
Chapter 5: EYE OPENER (Poems One to Thirteen) 91
Chapter 6: THOUGHTS (Poems One to Seven) 105
Chapter 7: INSPIRATION (Poems One to Thirteen) 117
Chapter 8: PLEADING CASE (Poems One to Six) 137
Chapter 9: THINGS SHE DO (Poems One to Fifteen) 145
Chapter 10: TRYING TO TALK TO (Poems One to Ten) 165
Chapter 11: WITH MUSIC (Poems One to Seven) 179
Chapter 12: BOOK ENDING (Poems One to Four) 191

INTRODUCTION

EXPLICIT THOUGHTS

To try is to fail, to accomplish something is to succeed

It's either risk it all, or not risk at all.

CHAPTER 1

EXPLICIT THOUGHTS

Morning Sex *(One)*

Morning sex be the best, be the best
Especially when you have a night of cuddling, kissing and touching
And you go to sleep with expectations of nothing
But you waken up to something like more gentle kisses
This time they are kisses between your thighs
Giving you an instant morning high
Just when you thought I was going to say goodbye and be off to work
I had to make it my duty to put in work before I go to work

Back to my gentle kisses while I tongue kiss my missus
Lower lips with a kiss that I know she will miss
While having a long day at work
I am glad I decided to put in this work
Eating you as my breakfast
There is no taste that can come next to this
Filling you with edible desires, this tongue will take you higher
Licking, sucking, kissing and touching
Then all of a sudden
You pour out, start cussing.

This started from nothing but a simple 'hello'
From Starbucks coffee flow
Something to wake us up and get us going
Now that you're done pouring and cussing
All of a sudden here comes something
Your legs are still spread, I put in the head
Along with half the shaft, because I just laugh
You know that there is more, we both can't ignore the pleasures
Of all of me inside of you, this is what we love to do.

Your pussy resists, I persist
And continue to presume to get all inside of you
The resistance is strong, you're tight and I am long
My head is so strong … your pussy is still pouring
This sex is never boring this unification is alluring as we're adoring.

Morning sex is the best
My mind is fresh with sexual thoughts while I go
In and out, we both scream and shout
You yell, "I need to get out!" and I yell "Not without!"
My finish and cumming, now here comes something
All of a sudden you're at it again, pouring on my little friend
Now back to my shout … I burst out in two
Different ways, I am in a daze
Your pussy always amazes me, your physical
Mental, spiritual flow is just crazy
Then you remind me you got to go to work, baby.

(Two)

Sexy professional, can I get next to you?
Can I tell you all my work-related dreams?
Let me have a private boardroom meeting with you
In-between all of these sheets
Unleashing the freak
That hides for the week
With the weekend to peak
Your higher heights of things that you like knowing
You wear things in spite
Because you know what I like!

(Three)

Dapussypleaserl: Hey, what's up, how are you doing today?
DIAMOND77: Okay
Dapussypleaserl: Did you work hard, or hardly work?
DIAMOND77: Both
Dapussypleaserl. So what are you doing now? Just relaxing?
DIAMOND77: Yeah
DIAMOND77: Trying to
Dapussypleaserl: Okay
Dapussypleaserl: Is there anything I can do to help you out?
DIAMOND75: Rescue me from this mess of paperwork I have to finish
Dapussypleaserl: Just take a flight, come over tonight
DIAMOND77: Okay
Dapussypleaserl: Allow me to get in your world, make change to you as a girl, sweep you off your feet with just one heartbeat
DIAMOND77: Please do
Dapussypleaserl: Take you to a different stage, put you on a high horse that fills with a blaze, the fires of passion
DIAMOND77: Do it now
Dapussypleaserl: Releasing in fashion, unleashing, the clashing of all good lashings of hits, while rubbing of your tits
Dapussypleaserl: Licks
Dapussypleaserl: Kissing of clits, even playing with whips
Dapussypleaserl: But first you must tell me are you able to do this?
DIAMOND77: Okay, yes I am
Dapussypleaserl: Are you going to put your cam on?
DIAMOND77: Yeah
Dapussypleaserl: Okay
DIAMOND77 camera starts

Wet Dreams *(Four)*

Can you imagine having a wet dream, but it seems so real?
Just think of being at home, just lying in your bed, falling asleep
Your man is away, off to work, and all you can do
Is think about him while he is gone
So you watch TV for a while and wait for him to get home
And then he calls to tell you that he'll be working
A few hours more than he thought
So you try to stay up a little bit longer to wait for him
But you start to nod off on the couch
You get up, cut the TV off and put some soft music on
And go back to the couch to wait a little while longer
Only to find yourself nodding off again and thinking of him
Sure enough, you fall asleep with him on the brain
You start to toss and turn and then you settle down
And a picture of him comes up in your dream
Freshly oiled down, pumped-up body glistening
Then you see him pick you up, take you into the room
And place you on the bed
After he places you on the bed, he begins to kiss your calf
And starts working his way up your thigh ...
And just over the ass cheek, onto the spinal cord
Then up the back to the back of your neck ...
As he does these things, you begin to get moist between your legs
And start to open them
Yet he closes them and continues with what he was doing
Kissing the back of your neck
He moves your hair over the other shoulder

And then starts working his way back down the spine on the left side
He gets midway down your back
And kisses that spot that gets you gushing wet
And you start to pour your juices all over the bed
Still asleep, you try to turn over, yet he stops you
And kisses your ass again
And then your bootie, your pussy ...
He licks once, just to get the juices flowing
And they start up again, all over his tongue.
The juices pour out and he licks them, and this time he touches the clit
To get more of a response from you
He turns you over, places his face over your clit
And starts to suck and lick
And whirl with his tongue
Then he places his tongue in your nest and you cum all over his face
Yet he still does not stop ...
He's licking, sucking, tongue fucking, until, until, until ...
You have your orgasm in his mouth
And you are grabbing his head
Only to realize that this was not a dream
Your man came home to fulfil your needs
Wet dream, wet dream, wet dream, wet dream, wet dream!
This is not just a wet dream
It's a dream that doesn't seem to be what it seems ...
Because it's not a dream: It seems like what it seems
Wet dreams.

Maybe One Day I can Have You For Dinner *(Five)*

Maybe one day I can have you for dinner
That would be nice ... you can come over
And I will have something for you to eat before I eat you
Whatever you love to eat, that will be your treat
But first I would like to see your feet
Get comfortable, that's how I want you to be
You over here with me
I see that you're looking tasty as hell
It's like I'm a man who just came from jail
I've been waiting just to get you in my cell
For a few hours.

Long talks over the phone got me praying
That you for dinner will not be that far along
With all that you say, telling all your friends
My relay laps around your body with my tongue
Massages your body and gets you numb
My dick and its trembling, and all of its enlarging
Got you forgetting about all your problems
Solving all my hunger, starvation …
That's why I want you in my plantation
So that I can rule your pussy sensation.

Maybe one day I can have you for dinner
At that time I will be the winner
With whatever your milky way pours
I will devour your center with my tongue once it enters
That day is soon to cum
By then you will be dinner for one
Then you will know more about this one
And how I feed off your cum.

Explicit Thoughts of Things I Want to Do *(Six)*

First I want to captivate your mind, tingle your spine
Then I want to know you're mine by knowing what's on your mind
The explicitly tricky mind-span of a madman
With thoughts in his hand of how to take over the land
For his woman.

Creating, captivating, illustrating things that were
once an illusion but became a solution
To the pollution of those who interact with delusions
Of the modified life of me trying to make you my wife.

An explicit lifestyle like … now knowing and
showing you where we are going
Things that have yet to fall in place are still
things for us to chase (better living …)
Thinking, pondering, cogitating where I am taking
This whole life for us two
And how the center of everything revolves around you.

Of, of, of stressing the fact that you and I can't relax
We must work hard to keep up this honor
In which our lives will be upheld
For our souls to prevail.

Things that can be looked past, from the past to the present
With you as my present
With explicit thoughts of the future
Because we are a few just people.

The explicitly clear thoughts of my mind
Lead me to redefine the thin line of threading sometimes
Weaving these physical fabrications, mending bad habits
Working towards our advantage
Of the explicit that explicitly defines the
simplicity which brings me to know
Explicit thought of things I want to do just to bring you closer to me
And become a part of you
This is just a start for you.

(Seven)

If I have sex with you and you don't enjoy it
Or feel some kind of way, then something is wrong with you
Either you can't love anyone or you have never been loved
Because my sex isn't that *good*, it is that *great*
Because I don't just have sex with you
I fuck your mind, I tingle your spine
I make you feel it when I come in from behind
And that's with only half of the thought in my mind
If you allow me to touch you, it will feel like I handcuffed you
Your brain will self-destruct two or three times as I enter your mind
With thoughts of these lines while I finish on time
('on time' meaning 'cumming')
And you going heavenly places that I am showing you
With these words we are going until the ends of Earth.
So if you have sex with me and you don't enjoy it
There is a problem we both need to fix.

(Eight)

Magic clit, is that what they call it?
How many men have spoiled it?
Touch it, tease it or even PLEASE IT?
Hopefully there is no one at this time
I understand that to do work for her is a full-time job
I would just like to know, are you taking applications now?
And did the last person put in his resignation
And how does it taste?
Sweet like a Haitian mango, that is
And do you have any kids?

I was told in life that the kids add on to one's history
And the taste of how it's supposed to be
So being that you have a magic clit
Something that every man wants to get
Can I someday find out more about this, and if you shout quick?
Or would you rather be pleased with some dick?

Can't forget; what is her shape/tone/complexion, and is she fat?
With a big hood for more protection
Oh yeah, and which do you prefer … fingers, tongue or penetration?
Or even all of them?
So magic clit, please tell how is it that I can
Get with
That magic clit?

EXPLICIT THOUGHTS: *(Nine)*

Please allow me to take this time to bring a point to notification
Throughout my life I was never blessed with the
aim to throw a ball, or the gift to catch one
I can barely dribble, or shoot a basketball
like a black man is supposed to
Those things have I not been blessed with
But another sport, which is one of the hardest to achieve
I feel that I have come close to mastering
And that is the sport of sex.

This graceful, but aggressive task is one of the
hardest things for a man to master
Keeping focus is one of the hardest things to do
But whenever my eyes steer toward you
I never tend to lose focus on what I would like to do
My goal is to make you cum in the worst way
The things I want to do are innumerable
So allow me to show you
My worst way imaginable.

EXPLICIT THOUGHTS: *(Ten)*

Showing off your prize possession is what got me wet
Mind is rushing, body is gushing, touching myself
I need to do something or get some help
From someone to tame this feeling that I'm feeling
I want to spread it all over your body and put it in your head
Letting you feel what I am feeling
Know that it is real
Keeping you in my trap made of steel
Not allowing you to break out, but only letting you scream and shout
Showing off your prize possession got me
thinking what to do next again
Try to get you over my house, so I can make
the bed squeak like a mouse
Your prize possession got me thinking what to do next
And your prize possession got me thinking what to do
next, and do next, and do next, and do next.

(Eleven)

Take down, hot sex wrestling
Argument, pushing, pulling, heated convo
You're right, I am wrong, you're wrong, I am right
Then
Make-up time
One touch leads to a kiss, like this
Lips to lips, then half-naked pushing over the bed
Then you hit your head on the pillow
Bite it while I touch you
Taste you with a facial
Soaking wet, just how I love to enter
Get in your center
Motions of a ruff stroke for a few minutes as I keep you close,
Turn you around, tie you down, I ain't playing around
Now I knock you down just with my cane now
Cumming together
Endless moments are forever.

Complexity *(Twelve)*

HIM:
Complex with me
Intricate ways and complicated days have
hazardous nights, I guess this is your life
You diminish and replenish the feeling of candor
You are like dry sand on a hot day, you're hard to get a hand on
Your relations are inundating, this is all from your creating
Kəmˈpleksədē ... why be so complex with me?

HER:
I am complexity
I will not allow you to get next to me
You will be graced with my presence
Only to feel the effects from our sexual encounters
This is all I will allow for us.

I know it sometimes makes you mad
Being that the heightened sexual experience
Is the only time I make my appearance
When the night falls and my sexual urge brawls
No one needs to know who I am
What my lifestyle is like now.

A few seconds have passed
Now it's in the past, no need in trying to make this last
I only come for two things
To cum and to have an orgasm
So if you can't fill the order, then we have no order
And this is disordered.

I have no time to waste, I want this pussy in your face
And your tongue to touch on one place
I want you to lick and suck my clit
In such a profane manner

That I yell out the right answers
Then I want your stroke to hit the spot
Make me become a Jamaican and yell out 'blood clot'.

I don't want, nor do I need more
Your thoughts of a relationship are not what I have in store
I am a successful college grad
Your sex might be the best I have ever had
But you are not what I want
So with my complexity, I will continue to hunt.

HIM:
So why mislead and continue to deceive, when you are what I need?
I am not what you need
I am what you *want* … your sexual urge is just a hunt.

HER:
Soon you will grow and know that playing
with these cougars is all for show
So put on your big boy pants and eat this pussy up to advance.

HIM:
My sex is not for sale … I have sex with you with the intent to prevail
Into your heart, with sex being the start
I guess these are a young man's thoughts
I guess these are a young man's thoughts
I guess these are a young man's thoughts.

Complexity has been so complex with me
That I have realized the real lies I was telling myself
That I am a young man and I am not advanced enough
To deal with this older woman's
Complexity.

To Whom This May Concern *(Thirteen)*

As of now, you're in an endless chapter in life
You're at home, lying down in your bed
Getting honey licked off of your whole body
Starting with a small amount placed on various areas of the body
I am starting to lick your toes, beginning with your right pinky toe.

As I savor each succulent moment, I advance to your ankle
Gently caressing your foot at the same time
Slowly moving up your leg, caressing each part while moving along
Just passing your knee ... now slowly sucking on your thigh
I savor this hardy portion of meat for a moment,
Then I work my way up to your pussy mound
I gently kiss your lips one time
Then I repeat the same process on your left leg
When I finally reach your pussy mound
I begin to eat my savored delectable.

In the process of eating, I add more honey
To enjoy the succulent flavor of my meal for the moment
Caressing your voluptuous clit with my tongue
And squeezing your nipples
You begin to become aroused
As I passionately place my finger in you
You start to loosen your tautness; squeeze, from your lips
And allow one finger in
Upon penetration of your love jonez
I find your G-spot and fondle it
Till your explosion of cum pours out of you into my mouth.

As we both reach orgasmic feelings never felt before
We adore the chapter and the time that was spent
Then the chapter came to an end
Only for a new one to begin again.

Yours undeviatingly,
Shazardes G. Richards

CHAPTER 2

FEELINGS ABOUT A RELATIONSHIP

Dear Doctor *(One)*

My imagination has hesitation when it comes to you
It's not the thought of how to, it's the thought of what to do
What to do to please you; mentally, spiritually, and emotionally
Ones' cognition get lost.

The influence and credentials
That you present to the people
Is only a small portion of what we still get lost in ...
The magnitude with no attitude shows gratitude
For how you were schooled.

You have me hesitant with my words; they're slurred—seem absurd
Brain freezes then sneezes to the jumpstart that's needed.

The immaculate thoughts that cost me seconds
Will not cost me hours
Because you are a blessing I want to devour
You are every good sculpture that can be framed in a picture
The sculpture of my dreams that I want to give everything to
This love ... all my money, maybe for housing a family.

Please allow me to hand to you
The right to passage
So we can pass this time, each second, each moment
I want us to own this process of endearment
I pray that you don't fear this, just please continue to hear this
Be my all, and allow me to be yours.

I'll give you any of your wants and needs
Give me time and I give you my word you'll see
Even if it's a want, you will get it
With the supporting system that we will enact
No outside perpetrator will ever attack.

Be sure to tell me as time goes by, so that our relationship can grow
And we never lack the love thereof, because
I will always be on guard for you
Let this love help to keep us true
So that any attacks never get through
This fortress of love I have for you.

Yours truly,
Shazardes Glenford Richards

P.S. Now that my heart is on the table, can
we have a mutual exchange?

(Two)

My thought and effort goes without stressing
I need this human being, without even seeing
And knowing her
Her beauty is just showing
But there is more to this
The more is?
You
She
Thee
Only one I need
My all, my everything
That I can imagine
My imaginable, yet unimaginable, I can't fathom you …
You're here in the flesh, I can only try to say what's next
To come from my mind, you are beyond divine
You are the most honest, beautiful, intelligent
I am just hellbent
On words
You are the goddess that I've heard of and I feel I deserve … in life.

I will get my chance to get to know you
I only pray you allow me to show you
What my worth is
Because humble like a kid
I assure you my worth will rise to the occasion.

For you I have been saving all my efforts of love
The love of family I lack thereof
I come with no extra packages
I have no kids, no one running behind me
Because all I need is you to find me
We need to grow into the family that the both of us want to have
To provide for our kids better than our parents provided for us.

Instinctive thinking, this allows us to think
And know
For our children to be better then what we are
And what we have become
We should be one.

I only pray our future holds the beauty of your dreams
You are my dream made into reality
My thought and effort
Came from a few losses
And the thought that I must have you at any cost.

(Three)

What is it I need to do in order to change my life for YOU?
You are my everything
You are the song I sing
You are the whisper in the night
You are my guiding light
Everything I do, I do for YOU
I would kill, steal and even drug deal
The endless things that I do, I do it all for you.

What Pain Is *(Four)*

You don't know what pain is until you know love
Love can be like pain
Pain in your veins
Pain can drive you insane
Insanity can be shown outside and hidden within
Until it comes out
And love makes you shout
With joy or pain
Then you will know what love is about.

Is that the love that you know?
Is that the love that you show?
How is it that you know pain?
Has pain driven you insane?
Has it burst in your brain?
Or is that the love in your veins?
That is equivalent to pain?
BECAUSE one way or the other IT'S ALL PAIN!

(Five)

The feeling I am feeling about being head over heels
Is just an appeal to how I feel
Words can't explain how you are not the same
To what I had, or what I might have ...
Your radiant beauty is a universal collision
That I didn't envision
I never knew I could be taken by storm
Just with everything that is above your arms
You have the brains and beauty
Along with the composite of a booty
All things that captivate, I meditate, you highly elate me
Just the thought of being in your presence
Makes me silently pray for the day
That I can walk into you again
Just to become your friend.
I've traveled and lived on both coasts
Just with hopes
Of getting close.
Knowing that we crossed paths
But didn't see each other
Alas, how is it we can be so close
Yet I am missing you again thus far?
I feel that the powers that be are working against me
Because all I can see is you with me
That woman that is to be the other half of me
The one I'm yearning for, the one I can adore
The one with who I can say, 'I don't need more'
All because you have everything in store
I still want and need you
I need to receive you
I need to believe you
I need to heed you
The words you state are the innate
Conscience of my moral state

Mind at ease, you don't just appease
You influence
Your endurance has the strength of a hundred lionesses
Yet you cuddle me like a cub and treat me like a king
Who is above any and all
That's why I continue to fall
So, until I am able to make you my all
Life will be like an endless fall.

Yours truly
Shazardes G. Richards

Why? *(Six)*

Why am I wasting my time?
Why am I?
That is the question I must ask myself.

There is something about you that makes me doubt you
I can't point it out due to the fact that you act
It shows me something you lack.

Is it the convo? Or the strange men in your convoy
That make me deploy
My senses and heighten my fences?

Maybe it's your pairs that I fear
Being everywhere at all these ballers' parties
Being real sociable
But then again, that's how I noticed you.

It was that time, that place, that high end space
Filled with drugs being spread like love
That naughty totty in the party
Making out with everybody
Yes, your best friend that I didn't notice until we began.

What I thought was a relationship
That was just a ship
That had a big chip out of it
Buoy …

I am glad I can see now
Slowly sinking, now I am thinking
Why am I wasting my time?
I stop and rewind and then I feel fine
Because I noticed I didn't really waste that much time
Just a few days, weeks, months
To realize you are a front.

(Seven)

The beauty of life sits with you as my wife
Even though I'm losing my future wife
It's the end of a life
A life of which could have been made better
With children, houses and the comfort of forever.

Seeing and knowing what life has been showing
The clash of outgoing minds …
Knowing that we are meant to be in unison with each other
This adversity! You're really just hurting me
And my feelings are falling apart.

You say that we are through and I know what to do
But I can't get it through the thickness in my heart
I just need to say goodbye
And let us fall apart.

I will respect your wishes with sincere kisses
So, goodbye to what we had
Hello to what we will have
A new future, a new start
Now that it's done, it was all just for fun
And a shattered glass is in place of my heart
The beauty is lost, a hopeless cause
Sitting with you, I wish it was
Just beginning.

(Eight)

HER:

You said you loved me and it's hard for me to believe it
I've cried because of your actions and couldn't tell you why
Love feels wonderful, it isn't confused,
Actually it's very matter-of-fact.

I have never allowed anyone in my space
That would have suggested that my heart
Was with anything, or anyone else
When I was in your presence.

HIM:

How is it hard for you to believe
When the things I do are what we perceived
The future of you and the future of me
Together or apart, we know where to start
My love isn't just words
They are the verbs
That my life speaks of.

HER:

Your love is a verb and it has moved me in so many ways
What it has truly shown me is I've never been loved at all
I have experienced lust and obsession
But never truly love … until the day you first left.

Your verb, your love … it moves about
And I've had to learn to allow it to flow in and out
When you leave you always take a piece of me
But when you come back you don't have that piece with you …
Where did you take it?
Who did you give it to?

HIM:
I gave me to you because that's all I know how to do
To turn my love into a living and breathing thing.

HER:
You said you loved me, and I had to act as if you said
"Something flew over your head,"
Because love to me, and love to you, are very different.

HIM:
The love that I have is different from any other
Person you might have had, or will ever have
I have been selfish and reckless with the love
I have shown and displayed to you
But I have become wise in my decisions with you
You have taught me how to truly love and to not be selfish.

HER:
You have truly shown me that love isn't
Obsessive or controlling, it is allowing...
And I allowed you to flow through me
How I've allowed you to!

But when I get a glimpse of who and what you turn your attention to
To be honest, I feel devalued
Love to me can only be loyal ... love enhances what already exists.

HIM:
Sexually, I have tried to be loyal
Mentally I have tried to be, but I can't because
Of what I see for you in your future.

I know that if I really display all the love I have for you
I will stagnate your growth
And that's not what I want to do
I want to always influence you
To rise to the occasion so that you can be
The woman that you are craving to be.

HER:

Sexually, you have abandoned me
You have left me in the cold to comfort and console my soul
My hand isn't your hand
My mouth isn't your mouth
My arms are not your arms.
You don't feel this pain.
Mentally, you have done the same.

HIM:

You knew I was broken when you first laid eyes on me
You could see the cracks in my smile
I thought in my brokenness we would become whole.

HER:

I understand that my future has called me
And when I ask God for you, He says this cannot be
All that I wanted is coming
You have my heart, my body, my mind.

HIM:

Love, to me, is there when you need a shoulder to cry on
And I would never allow time and space to linger
Like a dirty rag in a sink
Thinking back to these dirty rags in the sink
You are the only woman outside of my family
Who has ever washed my clothes.

This time and space between our face
Doesn't stop this shoulder from being here for you
It just allows us to grow closer when we are together.

HER:

Your love has given me security
I have allowed your strength to propel me
You look at me like I can do anything
I cannot believe that you mean so much to me.

Love hurt me to my core when I was a child
My inner child laughs because you exist
The old woman in me has stories of passions untwisted
Now, standing alone, all I can do is shake my head
Because my love remains.

HIM:
We will always share the same childhood feelings of love
And our losses
Parents getting divorced
Broken homes with alcohol
And drugs alone to fill the void
We have risen to the occasions
And not been subjected to the devil's cravings.

HER:
These pains are the connection from our conception
Love lost
Mothers tossed
From drug addictions—why can't we simply
See past all that we thought?
Be for one another like we wished we would be
Love said to me, he would pick me up for the weekend
And never showed up.

HIM:
As we move past the list of daddy's last words
We heard so many times
It still adds to the caption of what we missed and need
But only our Heavenly Father can give us to receive.

HER:
God himself has filled the holes in me
And I still ask that you do the same
I'm complete
I'm whole
And I've learned that I'm more than any story told.

HIM:
My father's words
Were that love was getting back together
With my mother
So we could 'be a family'
And it never happened.
I prayed as hard as I could.

HER:
At times my prayers were never answered
So I began to lose faith
But as I grew older, I realized that the time, place and space
Were not what the Most High wanted for me.
Now, with knowing that
I can say I have risen to the status of which I am supposed to be
And I am thankful for it.
When you say you love me—that's what I expect
And that's usually what I get.

HIM:
I know I have disappointed you in the past
And I will again in the future
But let me explain
If I give myself to you, I will stop you from being
that person that are supposed to be?
You are the woman for me
And if you be the woman for me
Then the career you are working on will not come to fruition.

I want a family
You have a family
And any additions to that will subtract from this beautiful ...
entrepreneur
comedian
actor
hostess
motivational speaker
mother

sister
paralegal
manager

The list continues
Because I can't name all that will be lost
From having me as that other part of you.

HER:
You can list, jobs, titles and careers
But love surpasses goals and dreams
Love flies higher than any goal you could ever dream of.

You keep running, looking for all that I am
One day, you will look around and figure out
that we could have had it all …
If you just believed.

On the other hand, I will love you because you are
The closest I've come to perfection
And I'm grateful because you have shown me—it gets better.

HIM:
Better isn't the word for what you will get
While I formulate these words, tears run down my face
When I realize the biggest loss I will ever take in life is YOU.

I can only hope to continue to linger around
To get a glimpse of what you are soon to become
And that your shine flows downhill onto someone like me
Because the Most High only knows
That I have the knowledge and power to inspire
But self-motivation and inspiration I lack
Because of so many failed attempts.

You are my motivation, inspiration, key to my meditation
Knowing that you are on my side no matter what
Helps me continue to grow and build.

HER:

If my inspiration needs to roll downhill to reach where you seem to be
It will arrive dirty and tattered
Beaten and battered.

Why would you allow something to fall from
The table and wait for the scraps
When I would love to spoon-feed your
Motivation, inspiration, love and hope
From the juices that flow from my body straight to you?
So love, to me, has been many things, but
So far it's never been truly mine.

I will continue to explore the love I have inside of me
And hopefully one day someone will see and match it
And allow magic to engulf us both
And if I never experience it, I can truly say
That I've been cared for by you in so many ways
On so many occasions
And for that I am truly grateful.

HIM:

As I bow out and take my steps back to hide
I can only hope and pray that the love will stay
Even if it's not in a sexual way
That is the only way I feel I can get you to stay
Because when I lose you, I lose a part of me.

HER:

How can you lose what I have given so freely, so desperately?
I have asked you from the beginning of time
To take my love and hold it there
You ran, you always hide ...
You step back and I think
Why do you come? Just to up and go?
I told you, you take a piece of me every time you leave.
What happens when I'm no more?

Let's Run *(Nine)*

Let's run this business together (relationship, business)
Let us join in a partnership that will lead us on a trip
Into a life which will give us a share of the stake
From the greener grass to take
Which our love will not break.

Let us run multimillion-dollar corporations
So that we can get our fixation
Of cars and kids, the beachfront estate
If that's where you want to live
Or even in midtown
Our dreams cannot be let down.

Let our minds build as one
A little boy or girl from out of our bodies will come
Let's clear a path
So that they can follow fast
And never end up last.

The unification of these two nations
Will lead haters to frustration
On our achievements
On where our 'bbbbbb's* went.

*Businesses[1], blessing[2], between[3] this bipartisan[4]
with you as my best[5] friend
Beloved[6] other
With you as my lover there is no stone to uncover
We will break down walls
Be triumphant over them all.

That's why we need to run this business together
So that we can look back at those who said never
Never see them together
Never see kids with them ever
Never see a future in their business.

What they don't know is that we don't need to show
Our business
Let us run this business together.

(Ten)

Am I too stupid to pay attention in life
To what is happening to me?
Do I not see what is going on with the females I am dealing with?
Seems like everyone is out for one thing or another
Most are out for money
Others are out for fame
And some are out just to play the game
With your emotions, that is …

Either way you're going to lose
If you let yourself get too involved with someone
And they're not feeling the same as you
You're bound to lose at every relationship
Things are different
Today it's money
Tomorrow it's fame
The day after, it's games.

Very rarely do you run across someone
Who is willing to accept you for *you*
And deal with your problems as if they are their own
Some of the hardest things to do in life are to find love
Make a lot of money
And stay out of jail
If you're a black man, that is …

This is why I ask myself how is it that I always
Lose when my heart gets involved
One reason is because as a man I fall in love with my *eyes*
And I guess I can't get a woman to fall in love with her *ears*
This is what happen when you try
To be an honest guy
You always finish last.

Maybe one day I will learn
Not to let my heart get involved
And my problems will be solved
These different females will dissolve
And I will have one main focus, and life will not be so hopeless
Because you are my awakening notice.

But until then I can't let my heart get involved
Because I will lose
And all my problems will come back and be unsolved.

(Eleven)

Glad to see you come, hate to see you go!
I am always glad to see you come into town
I'm like a child at a carnival on a merry-go-round
I only get to get on every once in a while so I
Must enjoy the time that was spent
The ride lasts for a few minutes and then it comes to an end
Except the ride with you is with my heart
I'm relaxed and at ease because the one I love is in town
So I feel more at one with myself.

I get to share these feeling that I have for you
For the few days that you are in town
Then the unthoughtful, dreadful thing happens
You know the worst part about your coming?
You *leave* ...
And all my feelings get put up on a shelf
In a book no one knows about, but you.

You are the only person who knows which book
And the exact page to get my heart from
And set it free for a few days, which feels like a few hours.
Why is it that you do this to me?
Why can't you stay and let my heart go free?
And just become one with me?

You know I hate to see you go
And the next time you go, please, please hurry up and come back
So that I can end this merry-go-round heart attack.

(Twelve)

Your skin tone and complexion are a vision of perfection
That beautiful brown skin has me willing to sin
My lustful thoughts are to give, at all cost
Your shoulder length hair has me up in the air.

Tantalizing eyes have me weak in the thighs
My admiration has me hesitating
Hyperventilating
Waiting for a real date again.

All I do is try and spend time with you
I try my best to capitalize on the time
But you're limited to mine.

I am all hours and ears, willing to give it all to show I care
You are busy and your lifestyle has me dizzy,
Already I am lost.

And all we did was talk
I have yet to caress your beautiful brown skin
And to make you my best friend
I yearn to kiss your lips, that everyone sees
But if I kiss, I will be the one to miss.

The thoughts that run through my mind
Are willing to tingle your spine
Creep up from behind
Only if you allow me to get in your mind.

Allow me to lead the way
Because of you, my confidence will go through the roof
You have all that a man can ask for
Three 'B's ... BBB ... Brains, Beauty, and Booty
Your humble being enhances a man's seeing
With his hindsight.

Everything about you is perfection
In a beautiful brown complexion

CHAPTER 3

ANGRY

(One)

Their impregnation was in their minds
There, birth was through my lines
That came from my voice, which made you moist.

(Two)

I don't condone and I don't condemn
I am just a man that may have sinned
Some of my actions are not so akin, so I ask for my blessings
So that I won't do it again.

So how did the rest of your day turn out?
Did you cum at the thought of my tongue?
Were you pleased, seeing me on my knees?

How about a pout with some in and out
Getting all of your attention with all the things mentioned
Being my student
Having you in detention
Locking you up with furry handcuffs
Telling you stuff
That sounds so rough.

Giving you something that you can't get enough of
This is love, the sexual bug
It bites and it tugs on your nipples
And thug—
I mean girl in a boat that likes to float
And gets your attention with sexual things mentioned.

Licking and sucking will only lead to fucking
But you're telling me something without telling me something
Your body is shaking, the jolts are breaking
My tongue from your clit, and you ask
How do you do this? I'll show you again
And you love it again …
The jolts end with you cumming.

Are your sleeping with him or me?
Who cares?
I just want a taste to keep you in your place
The excitement starts to rush, then you just blush
Sleeping, so what?
I could never get enough waking you up
Just to play with your clit
So I can put you back to sleep
So you can dream about this.

ANGRY: *(Three)*

Just a thought for the day
Cum sit on my face so that I can enjoy your taste
The lovely juices that flow so elusive that have me conclusive
About what I should do with you.

My tongue goes left and right, your body goes up and down
I lift my head up just to spin you around, still hearing that lovely sound
While you ride my face
You're pouring cum out all over the place
I am lying and it's all in my mouth
Just a little drips out.

You began to ride faster, you are my tongue's master
I slip it in your ass
But you just say I'm nasty
Now back to the pussy, where it just got so gushy
You start to scream and holler, you're fucking me harder
I won't even bother to come up for air
A gasp here, a gasp there … that's all you hear

Now using my head to vibrate between your legs
The rush to your head comes back down to your legs
You're starting to shake, I feel the earthquake
And then you decide to have one
Orgasmic proportion is where your cum is lost in
Then you get up and leave
And say, "I had fun"
All I see myself doing is making you cum!

To Onika *(Four)*

Acknowledging her presence, looking back at her past
The three main reasons why my mother passed away, today
From what Onika taught me
Sickness, desire and poorest to aspire.

When I felt she was supposed to lead the way, she walked away
She allowed her sickness to take away all that brought happiness
The love and joy that she brings no longer was anything
The beautiful smile that she passed down to me is now always mad
I frown at things I should smile at, because this is what life taught.

My desire to aspire no longer takes me higher
Than these drugs
And my motherly love, of which I am missing
Settled kissing
On my forehead
So the love's dead.

Occasional talks of how to revert
For what it's worth, I don't think it will work
Some of the poorest lifestyles when I was a child
You wouldn't dare let us live in these horrible conditions
With your sickness came these premonitions
Mental sickness and health, lack of wealth, poorest of values
So jail is how I found you
Trying to teach from the outside to a teenager growing to a man.

Never talks of getting me home
Just talks of leaving me alone once again, to fend for myself
If I would have had a little bit more of your love
I would be something else
Finding myself and finding my way
At the age of 33, what can I say?
I need a woman's undivided attention
So that our children will never mention
Being left alone inside of our home by a person so intelligent
Yet mental capacity so delicate.

(Five)

How would it be to have sex with you again?
How would it be?
It would be a pleasure for me to see how bright your face will be
How our worlds unite and spark our lights
Sex would be, with you and me, a divine plan to kiss one's hand.

I've had sex with others
But being in a marathon love affair with you is just for lovers
That's why I am glad to be your significant other
At last I can kiss you, and your whole body, while giving you a bath
Let's see how long the sex lasts
How would it be to have sex with you again?
The only way I would know is if I can start off with being your friend.

Ring, Ring, Ring, Ring ... *(Six)*

HER:
Hello?

HIM:
Are you craving for a late-night saving?
Am I what you are craving?
Do you want me to be your late-night saving?
Do you need me to hit that spot and make it hot?
How about air it out after I clear it out?

Are you craving for a late-night saving?
From being unscathed in the heat of the moment?
Sounds good, don't it?
Does the bass cumming across the phone
Have you mad at being alone?
Are you still craving? Need my saving?

Allow me to come and save them
Or you, that is ... and your sexual personalities ... 'mizz'
Or should I say 'misses'?
How many different 'yous' need kisses?
Saving, craving, late night
Just tell me and I will get it right
So now that you told me
Allow me to mold thee
Into a perfect picture of a molded scripture
Of sexual bliss
But it starts with a kiss.

However before I do
Let me come right over and kiss you
Right on the small of your back
And your neck with just a hint of sex
With very little penetration
All of the other things I do
Are to contribute to your craving
For a late-night saving.

(Seven)

Would you love for me to talk dirty to you, or just make love to you?
That is the next thing that I'm thinking about doing to you
So tell me what do you prefer?

HER:
I prefer for you to do what you want.

SHAZ:
Well the things that I want
Are to talk to you and see how you're doing
Where you're going
This can give me an idea
About the way I would want to make love to you.

HER:
I see, are you ready to listen?

SHAZ:
I am ready to listen
So you can get into submission with this physician
Over long strenuous positions
Now that we are talking, we should be walking
Away in life, where life is so nice
Knowing that dirty talking leads to walking
And how it all starts from my intellectual parts
And how they became smart
How this leads to the start
Again.

Starting with simple kisses from wet lips
Back rubs and bears hugs, soft touches just above your clit
Love-clutches along with kissing your navel
It's hard to behave
Knowing that feeling of this dirty dealing
And tongue twisting verbal affliction on the brain
Giving your nipples an erection also does the same
For your little friend/clit.

Driving you insane, knowing it's not the same
From any of those lames
From your past … so what would you like?
Would you like for me to talk dirty to you, or just make love to you?
Being that you are now aroused and uplifted to that cloud
How does it feel now?

I'm only just getting started, let me help you undress
To create a mess
Of water flowing and mind blowing
Touching, kissing along your back with some whispering in your ears
Something that I know you love to hear.

HER:
Ahhhhh, the other spot right there …

SHAZ:
So now let me take you over here
Lifting you up so that only my face can touch
Sitting on my shoulders
So that we can become closer
Missionary position, your favorite
You mentioned that is where we will go next
That is the best way to have sex
But when we make love sent from the heavens above
We have to just touch, just by standing up
Having you ride me so that our bodies collide deep onto each other
That's how we became lovers
Moving to our third and final position

One that we all mention
Getting into a stroking position
One that we need not mention
With some long vigorous strokes
No wonder lovemaking is so close
So allow me to make love to you
Just so that I can show you want I can do
Just remember I am only talking to you.

(Eight)

Some of the things I've seen in life
Sometimes it gives me strife
Ready to take your life
From the things I've seen
Will make a shiny piece of metal gleam
Dull with a nasty sheen.

Seen people stabbed with a knife, it doesn't seem right
I've seen people take a life in the daytime
And walk away as if it's night
With not a care in sight
Some of the things I've seen in life would make you think twice
And ask, how come this life isn't always so nice?
And why is it that I have to live this life?

I often wonder and think
Do I need to see a shrink?
But even after seeing a shrink
I still wonder about some of the things I think
Just because of the things I've seen in life ...

Misery *(Nine)*

Misery loves company
Oh I hear it's supposed to
Misery loves company
Because there is no one to ever be around me
I am misery and yes, I love company
Him or her to share my pain
Put it in their veins
Help them dish out my pain
Make others go insane!

My company is like a bumble bee
Stinging you and spraying you
So every other bee is attracted to that smell
Now can you tell
Help spread the wealth, even if it is bad for your health
You've got to love me
I am like something ugly.

I stand all alone as if I am in my own time zone
Life always seem to pass
But my misery will make it last
Some of my company know how to shake me off
But others just can't seem to get me lost.

Misery loves company
Oh I hear that is how it is supposed to be
So why is it that you don't love me?
Come to my warm embrace
Then let me slap you in your face
Hit you with this horrible taste
So that you can show it all over your face.

My company is misery … will you come and visit me?
I don't cost much, just a silent touch
Or just something to happen
All fucked up.

Come spend some time, I will help you unwind
I just hope you forget
So that the next time, misery will make you upset
Sometimes, I don't even need a reason
So come, my dear … I will share misery
Will you buy some for a buck?
Or just be miserable, with your luck
MISERY.

Precedent *(Ten)*

I'm here to set a precedent
My life is an act of its own
My precedent is forever shown
Take note on how things are easily overthrown.

As a ruler of my life
I set the trend of what's right
I leave trails and details on how to excel.

My precedent is the best of it
Showing you what's next to
This pedestal that I just stepped onto
Gets higher than being a don
Or a hood star from these words by far.

Listen and pay attention to all these things I mentioned:
Ruler, and precedent
Pedestal
Don
Yeah that's cool
D.ominating
O.ther
N.ations

This fixation of verbal correlation
Is part of the precedent of being
On this pedestal I am creating.

(Eleven)

Don't let them stop you
Something you should never do in life
Is let them stop you.

By letting them stop you
You are allowing them to stop the love that
Gloed through to your heart
And takes you to the places
Where they wish they could have a part.

Like when you are in love
And you and your significant other
Get into an argument over something trivial
And they tell you that he or she is not good
Wishing that they had that same person, or someone like them.

Or even if you grew up in the hood
Turned out to be good
Got a job that set you straight
You know they going to hate
Don't let them stop you
Only thing that they should be able to do is just watch you
And that's from afar.

Sometimes it's family or friends
Sometimes they hate and don't know it
They might not think it's in them
But it's just that they're not winning
Every part of life can be named as a game
Just that some don't play the same
Some always win and like to show off their fame
Others use that fame to inspire the same.

So don't let them stop you
If your score is high, and you are soaring
Don't let them slow you down or ask why
Just remember that you're not the bad guy
You're the one that took the time to prepare
And went straight in the field ready for war
Prepared.

Angry Black Man with a Black Woman *(Twelve)*

Bitch, you can't be serious
You must be delirious
Something got you precarious
Got you thinking that your thoughts are serious!

What the fuck got into you
Just a few days ago you was my boo
Now I'm ready to spill you
I don't even want to kill you
I just want to hit and run
That will be fun
I mean hit you with my car, that is
Then call the cops, so I don't leave you for dead.

Bitch, you can't be serious
You must be delirious
Just because you see me come into your favorite restaurant
That don't mean I want to haunt you, or even taunt you
I just wanted to get something to eat
Is there something wrong with me wanting to eat?
That spot just came to mind when I was driving down that line
Seventh Avenue, that is
I can't believe I wanted you to have my kids
Now I'd rather see you dead, or just run over by my car instead.
What the fuck would make you think that I want to stalk you?
Do I look like a stalker, bitch?

You can't be serious
You must be delirious
That friend you ate with got you thinking precarious
I don't know what's got into you
Something must be wrong
Singing some sad songs, I guess
Everything is going wrong.

I know you are leaving, going to Cali
I thought you would be gone by now
But that wasn't the reason why I wanted to eat at that restaurant
I just happen to be driving and got a craving
For some smothered chicken, rice and those greens
Do you know what I mean?
It's a nice spot you put me onto, thank you
But next time I know I will bring someone else with me.

Like I said, you can't be serious
You must be delirious
I just wanted to eat, what's so precarious about that?
Are you mad about me being there?
And not saying anything to you until I was about to leave?

And all I said was goodbye
When it came time for me to go, I didn't try to talk to you
I didn't try to make eye contact
You need to be slapped
I can't believe you would say something like that
Me, a stalker?
You better off at being a midnight corner walker
Selling your ass or something
This right here, I can't let this shit pass.

Bitch you can't be serious
You must be delirious
Because that email you sent me sounds like something
That I can't understand
At this present state in time
I am glad I am not your man
And I am glad I got the chance to say goodbye
To you once again.

P.S.
Enjoy yourself in Cali and have fun up in the valley
Be sure to get the bullshit out of your life
And stop thinking that every man does stuff in spite
And wants to make you his wife.

(Thirteen)

The anger and frustration
From the Lord's given creation
Leaves me hallucinating
Having thoughts of leaving
Of being deceived again
Why is it that I have you as my friend?
I need to ask myself again.

Its starts with the intellect
And its gets dissected
Into two halves of life
One trifling with the other
With you and me
I can't even fathom the words to say
They should be shown and displayed.

The anger that frustrates me
Leaves me at 'maybe'
What is it that could be done to keep us as one?

The unity that we were was ended because
The anger and frustration
From the Lord's given creation
Has me hallucinating
Fixating, hyperventilating on what to do about this sensation.

Just end this situation, that's what I'm tasting
It feeds it to the end, that's where I will begin
A new life, no more strife
No more you as my ...
Uh, I still can't say it, but I can display it
The end is close and near
Yes, my dear.

Only thing I'm waiting on is the lawyers
These papers, this date, time and table
I have never felt so disabled
I'm ready to end this fable
Or hell, of which I've been through just by being with you
Now that the papers are done we are ended as one
You are no longer my wife
You can get the hell out of my life!

CHAPTER 4

TWISTED EXPLICIT

(One)

As the New Year begins
My treading love ends
I begin to see past, the present … and look
Into the future of where we will be.

We've experienced the hills and valleys
Along with mountains and streams
Because this love wasn't what it seemed
It was supposed to be seamless.

As we turned corners, there was something new we had to address
You with him, me starting to love her, it was all a blur …
Just because we couldn't concur.

To allow ourselves to be on the same page
Just after the beginning stage
Months, weeks, days, hours and minutes go by
Without hearing from you
Or seeing a text message with you saying 'hi'.

The ball drops and it stops our clock
Ending what could have been the best thing
For each as lovers, understanding one another
Moving in cahoots, devising our excuse
To sneak away so we can go play
This treading love just ended today.

January 1, 2020
Goodbye to my past
Or what was present yesterday
Hello to my future
The new person I am about to get used to
As she gets ready to walk into my life
Hello present, modern-day, future wife.

Being Lonely Throughout Life *(Two)*

Being lonely throughout life isn't fun
I saw you today just a few hours after I said goodbye
I don't know if I was wrong
But I just was hungry and needed something to eat
I knew it was your favorite spot
But I didn't think you would be there this night.

I called you earlier to just say goodbye and bid you farewell
Even though we are not on good terms
You told me not to call anymore, so I won't
But I just had to say goodbye
It's funny how you can show someone something
And they do it often without you even knowing
And I guess that's what that was with the restaurant.

I saw you as I walked in, sitting at the table on the left
With your back to the wall, your friend in the aisle seat
We made eye contact when I turned around and took off my jacket
At that time you could have said 'hi' as well as I
But neither one of us did.

I sat there and placed my order
As you looked over your friend's shoulder
To watch what I was doing and who was I going to be eating with
But to your surprise, I ate with no one and didn't even stay long
Once I knew that you were there, I had it in my head to eat
But I lost my appetite
One I saw you, I just felt a sickness that I still have for you.

Sitting there being lonely throughout life didn't feel good at all
So instead of eating there, I told the waiter to give me mine to go
I finally got my food and paid the waiter
Put my jacket on
And as I was walking out, I turned to you and said
"Goodbye, Marmiko"
And you tried to act surprised that I was there.

It didn't amaze me that you would do something like that
But it leads me back to being lonely throughout life
If I had have said 'hi' instead of 'goodbye'
Would that have brought me closer to you?
Would that have made me the love of your life?
What would it have done?
I will never know
Because I guess I'm meant to be lonely throughout life.

(Three)

I bid my farewell and goodbye to love for you
Because I can no longer say 'hi' to lust
Lies you speak that break my heart
Are going to push us apart
They tear us away from the torn fabric of the relationship we had
And it makes you mad.

I travel, and I lost sight of our bigger picture
And sometimes I forget
But when faced with the reality
I committed a fatality of our morality.

Oh, how we are supposed to grow, bond and adhere to each other
So that we can continually uplift and be as if we are one?
But now I think it's done
I think I ruined everything we had
And I understand it makes you mad
The foreign women and flashing lights
Is what intrigued me on those nights
Now it's too late to make it right.

The only thing I ask is to be your friend
To continue to learn from you
Teach you, show you, how I should, or could do
That's why I am asking you
Allow me to be the friend I once was
This time, minus the lust
Just the undesigning trust that we have for each other.

Even though I am losing lustful ways
I am gaining a spiritual glove
Someone heaven-sent that is here meant
To help me see things through, just as I do for you
I bid my farewell and goodbyes to lust for you
And welcome my spiritual glove, that's new.

(Four)

Here is a promise to you.
I promise that if we end
We won't ever begin again
Also if I give you a kiss at the end of this
You won't be missed
So here is a kiss
You are no longer missed
This relationship is dismissed
And for sure I am glad about this!!!

You Are Surely Missed *(Five)*

I yearn for your gentle kisses, long eclipses
I miss the mornings with your bright smile
And the nights with your pretty brown round.

The days without your eclipses and gentle kisses
Don't seem the same
At night, I often find myself calling your name
And rolling over to hug and kiss what's not there
My mind wonders, why are not you here?

I often become lost and confused
On how we became amused with each other's attraction
The fatal ones that involves interaction
Of sexual bliss
Ended with our last kiss
From our last conversation
You are surely missed.

I'm Not in Town *(Six)*

How is it that I'm not in town when you are around?
I manage to keep myself away from you
Just to hide something that is true
You always ask, do I love you?

While that is something from me to you
I just don't think I should tell you
It's just too bad that I'm not there
I have to make it seem like I don't care
Because my cares
Are the least
Bit of anywhere
But there.

Pulling Me *(Seven)*

Pulling me wherever I go
You just keep pulling me wherever I go
Why do you constantly, persistently, artistically
Keep pulling me wherever you go?

I don't want to be where you are
I don't want to seem like my life is behind bars
Your life is behind bars
Because all you see is stars.

Not the stars in the videos
But the stars in Heaven
That of which you tried to excel yourself to
That of which you were banned from.

Left the most high, right hand from
You might be high in power, but your power can't devour
Or turn my good soul sour.

Why is it whenever I go
You keep trying to pull me down slow?
Liar: You the devil are not for me, so that's why I don't applaud thee.

Even though it's hard to ignore
I going to show you how to explore
Righteousness … because its right in us.

So stop pulling me; what you have is not what I want
I want healing of the soul
I want righteousness until I grow old
I want to see the promise
But what you want, you can't even be honest
So stop pulling me.

Seduction *(Eight)*

Why is it that you try to seduce me?
You know that I am a married man
The things you do are so seductive
The way you move your hips, your lips
The blow with your kiss, just got me like this:
Mesmerized.

You tantalize, I fantasize, now you got me in a panic
Why?
Your body is what I wish to have
But I, I, I'm lost for words
This is so absurd.

Seduction.

Why is it that you have no caution and you don't take any losses?
You're just up for the game
And don't treat any man the same
I thought I would be able to keep up, but I guess not
I almost forgot I'm married
But you say I'm not.

Seduction is saying ...
If you were married you wouldn't be here
So you mustn't care.

But I *do* care
I understand why I am here
I'm here to test my wall of love, that you fear

Your seduction can't break that wall of love
You are just eye candy that one fears
Men fear you because you are pretty to the eye
But are able to kill from inside
You are probably able to take me
On one of the best rides I will ever go on
But a few months later I will find out that my life is almost gone
So, seduction ...
Don't try and seduce me, because I'm happy and I'm married
Your seductive ways will not leave me in a daze
So go your own way
Your seduction doesn't live here today.

(Nine)

Through my life and despair
I couldn't be there
Sorry I couldn't be there
But I had to be somewhere, and somewhere is not there
Even though I wasn't there, please don't despair
But if you call another time
I will always be here
This is not a repeated motion, but a cyclonic potion
But if you give me your time and essence
I will surely be your efficient.

Sensual Kisses, Can You Be My Mistress? *(Ten)*

Sexually explicit, now let me kiss it
Tongue kissing your lips
Will have you like this
Head back as you relax
Thighs jumping while I am pumping
My tongue in and out of your pussy
I stop just to say, "Don't push me," (away that is)
As I kiss and suck
Your clit begins to become squashy, lips dripping
Tongue kissing, now you're spitting
All on my face
As I taste your juices while they flow
What I did, I do not know.

Okay, here is how it goes
We start with going out to dinner
Gentleman treatment as I enter
Your mind from behind, sit you down at the table
Tell you in your ear
I want to kiss your navel
While stealing a kiss behind your ear
You look back as if you don't care
I listen to your day, then I start my foray
Tell you how dinner was good
But you as my dessert is where it is
And you have something waiting for you at home
I can't wait to get you alone
As you enter the house, roses on the floor
Leading to the living room where candles are lit
A tablecloth on the floor so that now you can explore
Sexually explicit
Thinking back to what I've done
I only just begun
To use my tongue.

Money Taken *(Eleven)*

I am starving
I got no money
I am hungry
This feeling comes on me
What am to do?
Who am to do it to?

At this moment I don't care
My sorrow blessing I will share
With the next motherfucker
Who comes past here

My blood begins to rush
I start to say, "I don't give a fuck"
Here he comes I am going to get him
Middle-aged guy, dressed kind of fly
It's just a quick jook
Don't ask why
I need that money, that's why
He walks by.

Hit him over the back of his head
I think I knocked him dead
Nah, he's just out for the count
A couple of hundred dollars, that is the amount
Not bad for the night, didn't even have to put up a fight
But did alright.

Seeing and knowing the way I am going
I will need to be showing myself some more food
So I need a schedule
Because these small jooks ain't cool
So now line up a team
You know what I mean
One center
One power forward
One small forward
Me on point
And the other a shooting guard
Soon to come
Armored cars.

Don't Blame Me *(Twelve)*

I speak gentle words, the things I say are always heard
Don't blame me
For having sex with someone in your family
I only spoke which lead to a poke
Better yet, a swift stroke deep in her throat
Moving around in her uterus
It's you who guessed that I was the one
When it was her who came over for some fun
I explain the pain that drives you insane
About having sex with some of your closest friends
Yet still the same thing goes for them.

Don't blame me
I speak gentle words, the things I say are always heard
What's in the dark comes to light because
The light is only gone for the night
The sun illuminates some of my past dates
For you, as my friend, it becomes a bit innate
This situation, it's frustrating
So without hesitation, here is the elaboration
Of the situation.

Don't blame me
I just speak gentle words, the things I say are always heard
By those who become intrigued and ready to receive
Something for their sexual needs
It starts with a touch, then a kiss and ends up like this: Sexual bliss
Something they have all missed
Something that you might have divulged on
Just because a woman's pride is strong
That little, tiny hint is what made them want to present
Things that should have been kept in confidence
Yet your conversation finds it relevant.

So I am where I am because of these women
Sexual escapades that cascade what was in the shade
Are now in the light; we already discussed that for the night
Now things will never be alright, but it's alright!
This is a lesson learned, stripes earned
Sex with your friends and sister confirmed
Now our friendship is burned
And it's all because of them wanting their turn.

I only speak gentle words, the things I say are always heard
So don't blame me for what I did
I am just happy that none of us had any kids.

P.S.
Let's keep our dealings amongst ourselves
So that we don't intrigue anyone else.

(Thirteen)

I need permission
While having sex with you, I need to ask you
Can I have permission?
Permission to enter your heart
Permission to enter your body
Without anything to stop us from feeling each other
Permission for us to join our souls with prayer until we get old.

I need your permission for this new position
With tranquil ambition to lead us to a higher sexual definition
While I am inside of you, I will ask you to let me love you
With your permission, I'll heighten your sensuousness
Disable your defenses, show your consensus
That our love will become relentless.

Now can you defend this
Fight for a stronger future with two of us
Where we lost love from friends and family
That didn't want what we worked for
So their feelings we have to ignore
Because in your eyes and in mine, you are divine
And I wish I had you in my life for all this time
Now with your permission
I will continue kissing
That will lead me to all these things mentioned.

The Kitchen Sink to the Countertop *(Fourteen)*

BACK SEAT LOVING
PEBBLE BEACH
PUBLIC PLACE
MOVIE THEATRE
JUNIORS' BATHROOM
TRAIN CAR, LATE NIGHTS

You tell me what you would like?
Then I will write to YOU.
EXPILCITTHOUGHTS2020@GMAIL.COM

CHAPTER 5

EYE OPENER

Sinning is Winning *(One)*

If sinning is winning, why did it start at the beginning?
Why did the devil try to befriend them?
Sinning is the biggest lie the devil told the world
If sinning is winning, why is that?

Is it that's all we know, all the action we show?
How is it that we got this far? How can we
Stop from sinning tomorrow?
The Most High told me, "Stop sinning, because you're not winning ..."
I ask you, Lord, what are the things I need to do
In order to give my life to you?

"Follow the commandments!" is what he said
This will end the sin before it reaches ahead of your life
Stick to them and know them right
Continuously learn them so you can be a child of the light

So ...

If sinning is winning, that's what the devil told them
That's why they lie, cheat, steal and never need a purpose to kill
But it's time for us to change this ordeal
How can we win without sin?
To win without sin, it starts from within
Learning the laws and applying them all
Using them to your advantage so that you have a higher vantage.

(Two)

Infatuation
Led me to a fixation
With hopes of higher elevation
And our lives with no frustration.

But …
Understand my correlation
The future of us—not me, but we
Where I would like to be?
So, you tell me.

A life filled with traveling, luxury cars, the finest apparel
With the world as our playground
Are you willing to stay down?
After this bid, you will see how I live
Go half on some kids.

Working and making things right
Working hard, holding down two jobs
So that everything is in reach
As long as you don't allow a breach in our walls
That would be our downfall
And the best for them who want to see us fall.

I Don't Know You *(Three)*

I don't know you ...
You are who?
Who are you?
Na Na Na
I don't think I know you!

See, if I know you or I think I knew you
Then I would try my best to show you that I know you ...
But being that I don't know you
There is no reason to show you how, or why, I know you.

You keep saying I know you. but
I know you but ...
I don't have the words to prove or show you.

How is it that I know you again?
OH ... ohh ... ohh
Now I know how I know you!
I looked in the mirror the other day and I saw two faces
You, being the other, the psychotic brother

Now I know why I know you
You are the other me
The one that comes out only when I want to make a scene.

(Four)

I aspire to never retire
To work to get what I desire
To always be admired by those who want to get higher
My aspiration leads you to your admiration
Which gets you your fixation
Of your higher elevation.

So Beautiful *(Five)*

Have you ever seen a person
So beautiful in your eyes
That you just want to have them?

Beautiful in every and all ways
Intelligent, caring—with you the list goes on and on
For me, you are that person
It's just that I was late finding you.

I wish I could have you in my life
Because right now all I do
Is think about you.

(Six)

Shazardes G. Richards
Walking into your life
Phone: 347-627-5143

To whoever is reading this:

Don't let me past you
Can I be blessed to have your phone number?
Allow yourself to enter into my life!

Morning Robust *(Seven)*

Good morning
My robust smell helps liven your day
My sweet but bitter taste wakes you up in the morning
My distinctive smell can be smelled from rooms away
Most likely you know who I am
If not, my name is coffee.

I come in many different flavors
But *my* particular flavor is grown in the Blue Mountains of Jamaica
And ground down to a granular powder
By the time I reach your hands
I am placed in a cup
Diluted with 170-degree water
Dashed with cream and two teaspoons of sugar, preferably three.

Some prefer me cold, others as cappuccino
What do you prefer?

I'm drunk alongside of a delicious breakfast
With ackee and salt fish, with yam dumplings and banana
You might like me as a French vanilla or chocolate mocha
But when you narrow me down, I am still the same
My very special blend was grown in Brooklyn
And would like to know if I am the cup that wakes you up
If so, please tell me so
And I can have my robust flavors ready for you
Every day in the morning.

Yours undeviatingly,
Shazardes G. Richards

(Eight)

S.H.A.Z.A.R.D.E.S
SUCCESSFUL
HANDSOME
ARROGANT
ZEALOUS
APT/APTITUDE
RESILIENT
DEVIANT
ELUSIVE
SWAYING OR SEDUCTIVE

(Nine)

Early morning thoughts of you and the things I would love to do
Breakfast before work then after a long, hard day
Hot showers, while I devour your orgasmic powers
Then soft touches, while I massage your clutches.

I will tend to your pain from long standing
Endless thoughts of how I will manage, or orally damage
I mean ... bandage
Someone who I will love to handle.

What is it that you are doing to me? *(Ten)*

What is it that you are doing to me?
You got me messed up in the brain, going insane
Feeling as if life is a big pain
And still you got your love flowing through my veins
Is it you got me going insane?

What is it that you are doing to me?
I must ask you again
The things you do are so brand new
Never seen in the ocean blue
Or even in the orange skies
Or at midnight
Why?

Depth Perception *(Eleven)*

If my depth perception lead me to an interception
It means my deception has an inception
My conceptive thoughts are where I get lost
Arranged in the hazy mist
Clouded vision of interest has me senseless
Inceptive clues left by deceptive 'yous'
Along with 'whys' and intercepted 'byes'
The perception's depth
Is where we are left.

Confide in the Lord in Your Time of Trouble *(Twelve)*

Let no evil spirits break that link between you
And the higher power above you
Let those who say they love you, love with
Whole hearts and big smiles
Let them be the shoulders that you cry upon
And your heavenly father be the one you rely upon
To heal you and mend your heart, and to show you where to start.

Confide in the Lord in your time of trouble
For sure He hears you, He is the one above you
Send your prayers through His son, for he is the begotten one
Allow your friends to mourn with you
To help the pain, for their love is dear, and not in vain.

Those who are close, let this bring them closer
Let you and your family confide and decide together
Become wiser in this stormy weather
Let PSALM 23 also soothe your soul
Let MATTHEW 6:9 make you whole
Confide in him
He is who you should rely on.

(Thirteen)

As I listen to this song and ingest the thought of you
Considering the things I would do
Looking into the future, thinking about the past
Realizing by any means we will need to make this last
Endure the test of time
Allow our souls to intertwine and the caged hearts to unwind
Hoping to see you one more time.

CHAPTER 6

THOUGHTS

(One)

I can give mental stimulation with just an oral fixation
Or verbal correlation without any abbreviations
What is it that you like?
How is it that you need it?
What can be done to make it better?
In which way would you want the weather?

Expectations lead to creations
Without hesitation of you sitting on my face again
I mean just facing him
Him being I—the person you open up your eyes to
To help you realize that
The little spot on your thigh is where I place my ...?

Time
My head relaxing on your lap as we chat
You know about this and that
More so, that then this twisted this
With a kiss of your mental bliss
Now do you understand me, Miss?

P.S.
I am asking about your goals, or if you think
dirty and have dirty thoughts.

(Two)

Salutation to
Daily aspiration with connotation
Leads to elation, with less hesitation …
Highly impregnated.

Evaluation had me thinking about what you were saying
Inspirational words that flow throughout the Earth
That aspire and help take us high
Us being me, thee and anyone who comes into contact with *you.*

Allow your gift to be our continuous presence
That enlightens and heightens our senses
Takes us from being defensive
To be tranquil.

Your daily aspiration with no connotation
Leads to an elation
That helps me formulate this sensation
Of verbal stimulation.

(Three)

What are your thoughts about being the one that I love?
Your thoughts of being the one that I hug?
My thoughts are constantly about you
Small thing are constantly coming true
But the majority of things are still not with you.

I see a vision of us having a life
In that same vision I see you as my wife
Me constantly pushing
And those who hate, ambushing
But with these two highly intellectual
Undetectable, silent mind killers
Not only do we feel us, we feel the rush
Of us coming together
Evolving and solving all issues
Because we have no fear
We have yet to be, but soon to be THERE
At the finish line making it at the same time
So what are your thoughts of being the one that I love?

So, When Will I Know It's Time? *(Four)*

When will I know it's time?
When will I know not to commit the crime
Of trying to take away your heart?
I am just looking for a place to start.

Trying not to go back to my criminal ways
Do you remember how I was back in the days?
Robbing and stealing, sometimes even killing
The hearts of those I should love
Now I look for blessing from our Father above.

One blessing is to convince you to allow me to have a chance
Or just to converse, not even romance
Let me bring poetic words to your life
At least just for one night
When will I know?

(Five)

I wish that someday I could have you in my life
Call you my wife
Show you my life
Show you what's right.

I wish that I could pray with you
Stay with you
And say a few words or verbs
That will make you move to the suburbs
Hear things you never heard.

I wish that I could show you the world as we travel this Earth
I wish a wish that I wish would come true
I wish that I could be with you.

With all these wishes and hopeful kisses
Allow me to regress ...
My ego shows you a hero, or even a superstar
Because as your future husband, that's what I am.

I wish we could work on some kids
To have a beautiful family, with you!
Just like ...
Me teaching and guiding, showing our kids
That I wish a wish that you stay, after this argument.

There is always some bothering, leaving and toddling
The thought of dishonoring
Our loving agreement
That we both sought to have.

I wish that with that
I wouldn’t say this
Sometimes things do happen
But if I wish and pray I am sure that this will go away
So I wish a wish today
And that is for you to stay
And our problems to go away.

TOWER CRANE

High Life *(Six)*

Fifty floors up, towering over the world, looking down
Everyone looks like ants, putting these buildings together
People say I am crazy, I just say I am not lazy
I got to provide for my family, and this is what life hands me
These tools and this belt … this weather is what is felt
Freezing winter days and hot summer nights
As I put up a fight just to make ends meet in life.

Asking Myself, Can I have You for Breakfast? *(Seven)*

Allow me to have you for breakfast, waking you up with my tongue
Stuck in between places of which faces are only allowed to come
Do you remember me?
The tongue from last night, when I and your clit had a fight
I added whip cream to my advantage
So, somehow you couldn't manage
Back to you for breakfast, let me lick up my mess quick
Licking off the remains from last night
Added with some new ones, like syrup to heighten the fight
Circular motions with your cum potion
I mean *compulsion* of what this is—breakfast in bed
Now as the fight continues, I add to the menu
Just a little up and down, I didn't even start to suck it now
Fuck it
Sucking on your clit, your legs start to shift and shiver
As I deliver these repeated blows
Circles, up and down and sucking
You, curling your toes
As these minutes start to pass, you have your orgasmic blast
Now it's time for me to go
I am done with my breakfast
I got to get ready for work, though!

CHAPTER 7

INSPIRATION

(One)

What can I do in order to get to where I want to go?
What is it that needs to be given to get to where I want?
How do I show that my time and dedication
Have no hesitation?
And I am past the elusive thoughts
Of where I will end up
If I stop short
So I endure and strive … just to survive … must stay alive
By living and giving I am devising and compromising
Then realizing how surviving is a part of our lives again
They say you must give to get in order to have
A part of this brand that they call life.

Unadulterated *(Two)*

Life can be unadulterated
Things can seem so easy
Because someone has something that you don't have
You can always stop and wonder how is it that he/she can afford that
Or how did they get that?

Some of us always think, "Yeah they did some fast skim to get that"
And others think, "He must have worked hard"
Whether if it was selling drugs or using a jackhammer
They did something
Devised a plan that helped them to get what they wanted in life
And what they got might only be the start
They might be working to get more and bigger and better things.

Life can come to you as is
Or you can lead the way you would like life to take you
It's just like when you are young, and your parents ask you
What would you like to be in life, and you say, "A doctor ..."
If you start to prepare at that young age
To train to be a doctor
When you start, and get going on your goal
Nothing will stop you from your plans
Because it is imbedded in concrete
That you are going to be what you want to be in life
Because you work hard for it.

The same thing applies to a drug dealer
He sees big-time dealers in the nice cars and big houses
And he wants the same thing
So he asks that dealer, "How is it that I can get what you got?"
In some cases, if they are close, dude will tell him
And he will take it from there
He will learn that selling for someone else
He will not make much money

So he'll sell for himself, and get others to sell for him
He's in the business of selling drugs
But he learns how to maintain his re-up money
And cop more at a cheaper price
To make more of a profit and get more kick-back.

Now with that child that wants to be a doctor
If s/he is smart, willing to start to speak to doctors
And ask what books to read that will inform them
Of what they need to know about how to be a doctor
S/he will have a head start on the test that they will have in the future
This will prepare them.

Life is so unadulterated
That one of these two can be a millionaire before the other
But one with more risk than the other.

You need to ask yourself about your personal, unadulterated life
Am I a person that is in it for the fast nickel?
That is better than a slow buck
Am I in it for the fast money that has no longevity?

You must also ask yourself … am I willing to be a leader?
Can I set a path that no one else has set?
But yet
Still keep in mind that if you work hard for it
You will get it sometime.

Unadulterated
This is what life is to us
Some have it easy
Some have it hard.

(Three)

Black women deserve a black history month
Mothers, sisters and friends—they deserve it to the end
Without them, we wouldn't know where to begin.

They innervate, motivate, concentrate
They help us to maintain focus, yet keep us from being hopeless
They welcome us in their lives
Help us with our rise
They integrate us, they mentor us
They nourish us with their thoughts and harmonizing words
They influence us
Take us into their lives and become our wives.

Black women, you deserve a black history month
Without my mother, I wouldn't be here to make it, or say
That black women deserve a black history month
That is something I cannot front.

My mother was once crazy, still she raised me
To become a strong black man, that is what I am
She always helped others, even if they weren't children of lovers
And she made sure us kids didn't hang out on the street
And never minded giving us something to eat
She helped me overcome my past circumstances
Being that my father was never there
Without his influence, I didn't really care
For a female influence was always there
Because my mother always showed she cared.

So, black women's history month is something that I need
It's something that we should cherish indeed
Every man has a mother, every bother has a sister
They need a man who cares.

These black women became our mothers, sisters
And influence other women
They show that they care
We need them in our lives to help us from becoming undermined
We need influence, inspiration
Infections from the deepest, darkest, most creative
Most respectable women alive
So black women's history month, it's something we all need
It's something that, if I do get it, I will cherish indeed.

(Four)

The beautiful thought of intuition
Led me to recognition
Of you.

As I stare in a daze
The beautiful haze that intuitively blazed
The fire and desire of wanting to have you
For lack of better words, I want all of you
Mind, body … and for us to join our souls
And praise the most high until we get old.

Intuition, recognition, has its suspicion
That we can overcome with our rendition of love
When we become joined together by the Father above
With different ways of showing our love
Some things are farfetched; however
intuition will show me what's next.

So, Miss, what's next?
Is intuition part of your dialect?

(Five)

Successor, that is what I am
Capitalize, that is what I will do
Conqueror, that is who I will be
Because there is nothing that can stop me.

Adventures, that is how my mind wanders
Clueless, that is how haters slumber
Lifeless, lost in the abyss
Trying to catch me, however they always miss.

Life awaits me to take control
To get in the driver's seat and then to go ...
On my journey, with no need for an attorney
My goals and riches seem more than just pictures
And things that I want
It's all just a front
Portraits of physical things ... that's not what life will bring
Unto me.

Life will bring to me:
Freedom of thought, freedom of speech
Freedom to travel across the foreign seas
Freedom to help those within my presence
Whether it be just through words
To inspire them to get caught-up in life rapture
Or by showing them my before and after.

Successor, that is what I am
Capitalize, that is what I will do
Conqueror, that is who I will be
Because it is in me.

(Six)

My destiny brings out the best in me
With you as my destiny
You'll bring out the best in me
Timelessly, effortlessly.

We shall work toward a breath indeed
A breath of air on the lighter side of things
Of which the best life brings
You as the best in me, being my destiny
Showing, growing, illuminating, glowing ...
Building on our world, with you as my girl.

Life seems endless, the toughest battles are no stress
Learning from our past how to make things last
One day to look back at how we grew that fast
With words of supplication that planted information
With us from different nations
We conjure up a fixation
that
My destiny brings out the best in me.

I would hope that you internalize
Visualize
Mesmerize
But never capsize
Always capitalize on a prize which can be yours at no cost.

MY life can be for you
DESTINY can be what's true
BRINGS each other together
OUT of the past now into the future
THE world is what I will try to get for you, because you're worth it
BEST of all you are everything a man can want and need
IN beauty and brains, you have something to drive one insane
ME being selfish, only thinking of what your wealth is.

Intelligent, beautiful … what did the Lord do to you?
Blessed you
Then it's now on toward a future or family
My destiny brings out the best in me.

(Seven)

Just a few kind words, that's all you heard
Those words you heard help relax the mind
And take you to a new place in time
Help you to feel as if any problem can be erased
These words go from one end of the Earth to the other
And nurture in the process
For all that its worth
I love you.
Do you love me too?

These are the words that help to change the world
Whether it be by way of friends or enemy
We try to find common ground just so that our kids can play around
Can you say it with me?
I love you ...

You can be my brother, mother, sister or just my friend
I love you for all that you are worth
Even when we make each other hurt
Just a few kind words, that's all that you heard.

Can I tell you something in your ear, my dear?
I do, I do, I really do love you ...
It's more than just sex, it's what comes next
Are you ready? Here it is.

Your intellect, your introspect
And your beauty, it makes me always want to say
Just a few kind words
That's all that you heard.

(Eight)

I want to write tonight about my life
My life has been a day-to-day hustle
Trying to use my muscle, or what little I got
Can't stand to hustle, because the dealer is no longer in me
Trying to convert my life and find a wife and make things right
Have a family, raise my kids to do the things I never did
I've only seen a small portion of the Earth
The rest is out there to show me what it is worth.

I will write tonight about my life
Take you to sometime in the past where people got killed
Things got 'stealed' ... and some of us lost our vocabulary skills
Here is what's the deal
I live across the street from a park
Where the cops are afraid to walk in the dark
I live up the block form the waters
Where the gangsters take care of their orders
I'm also across the street from the stores
Where there is beer and liquor
And so much more
Anything you want, bet you I can get it
With just a look of the eye, a pound and a five
That will be the trick to how I survive.

Never said I was going to make things right
I just said I want to write tonight and tell you a little bit about my life
Well if you go around the corner
Then you will be in one of the worst places that you will ever see
Blood on the floors, kids playing
You got shells next to valves, taps next to cracks
I declare war next to the feared wall
You got jungles next to those bundles
Basketball courts next to where people hold court
Can you see where I'm coming from?

I'm from the place where guns beat like them drums
Bullets overcome and even cops run
Just take a few seconds and listen

I wanted to write tonight about my life tonight
Tonight is the night I make things right
Tonight is the night I try and save a life
Just by telling him what's right!

(Nine)

Can I invest in you? Can you invest in me?
Can we grow and build on this family?
So that we will see how our future will be?

From the time we met we shared a lot
Conversing on the things we want
To make our funds equate to the same
As the big spenders in the game
Our stocks rise and fall
That is when we go through it all
Knowing as time goes we will merge together
And make a higher gross
Combine all our assets
Formulate new corporations
In the process show that are willing
To learn this procedure of how love can be eager.

Can I invest in you?
Can you invest in me too?
Can we grow and build on this family?

A Letter and an Artist's Painting *(Ten)*

Allow me to scribe to you a written letter
About all of your gorgeous features
Stone-gray backdrop, leather and velour couch
Classic car painting hung on the wall
And your beautiful cinnamon skin standing out most of all
While you sit with your legs crossed
My painted/written vision gets lost
Mesmerized by your eyes
Tantalized with the thought of kissing your cinnamon thighs
That dress fits you best, four-inch peak toe heels
Are starting to give me the chills
Your hairstyle is amazing, pulled back, not leaving any shade
Bright, beautiful smile, glassy eyes

I am almost done drawing now
Your succulent B-cup breasts poke out
When your back naturally arches out
A slight twist of your pelvis, now let me expel this
The beauty that lies between your eyes
I'm mesmerized by your thighs
That only comprise the rest of your amazing surprise
Cinnamon tone, brown bone
I'm in awe while I draw/write this … alone

Black and Strong, So Nothing Should Go Wrong *(Eleven)*

I'm black, I'm strong so nothing should go wrong
My blackness defines my roots
My strength isn't just in my boots
It's also in my roots
The roots of my head where my locks grow and get big
Just like my kids.

My blackness isn't just my strength
My brain is the thing the Most High gave me to think with
That is where my true power is
And in my loins where I push out my kids
Nothing should go wrong because it's a well-planned storm
Fast and quick, yet all so swift
Good thinking is how I can do this.

The plan is to overcome
And pound on it until it's done
Or make use of it to make something new
It is my blackness that allows me to do what I do
It helps me to think so big
Because I got my street hustle along with my book muscle
So I'm black and strong
So nothing will go wrong.

(Twelve)

A start is a start, no matter where you start from
You have to start to find the finish
If you finish, then you know where you started from!

By knowing where you started from
You know how to do the process all over again if need be
If any mistakes happen or come your way
You know how to handle them just by going back to the start.

Sometimes, starting over can be a horrible ordeal
When you play your cards
In one hand you might get all aces and kings
And in the other you might get mixed numbers and a jackass …
That never goes together to make a hand!

Remembering your start is also hard sometimes
Because you go through so much
That you never want to remember again
However, that may be the best part about starting
The whole ordeal and mayhem that you go through.

(Thirteen)

What's on my mind?
A lot of things … mainly money
What's on yours?

Things that I want and need in life that friends can't help me get
Working for it will just be too hard
So what's on my mind?
Money.

What do I need to do? How can I acquire it?
Why is my desire for it?

What I need is some men's greed
Some break their backs, some have heart attacks
Just over that big paper stack.

What is it that it does to me?
It helps me in every way
From the headache of bills, to keeping family away
Brings about new friends and old enemies
So what is it that is on my mind?
Money: That's what, it's money.

Some pull fast jooks
Some end up dirty crooks
Selling valves filled up with dirty looks
Some bankrupt companies crash the stock market
Some hide it under their carpet
However, it's on everyone's mind
Whether it is in the front or behind
Money is on their mind.

So what's on your mind today?
I see that sad face
Are your bills backed up?
Your parents didn't teach you how to keep that money stacked up
That's what it is, it's not your kids
Money is what it is
It's always on my mind
That's what's on my mind
Money.

CHAPTER 8

PLEADING CASE

(One)

I would hope to never leave you
Just like I would hope you never leave me
I would hope that our lives can be bigger than your expectancy
Even if I wasn't there for much of your twenties
I would hope to be there for your thirties
To persistently walk with you into your seventies and live life swiftly
Allow me to catch up to you in life
And set a precedent with the thought of you as my wife
Wouldn't that be nice?
A doctor and a crazy patient
Trying to fill that vacant spot in their hearts
With just one place to start
Here, if you allow me to show that I care
I would hope that you allow me to be there.

(Two)

Roadway closed
Merge left while I daydream
It seems my mind schemes on thoughts of you in my dreams
The misty gaze, the beautiful haze
As I sit here stuck in this trance
You are my mind advance
Life-changing, mind-framing
Clear thought ranging for miles and miles.

We shouldn't separate now
There is so much we have to accomplish
There is so much we have to accomplish
(I come out of the trance)
I stop and look where I stand
Back in a trance.

Roadway closed—merge left
You left me better
Yet, you're leaving
These good dreams are deceiving
My feelings are conceiving
Now life isn't what it seems again
Back to the horror story of being single
Vivid dreams from when I mingle

Now I know why I dread the dream of being single
Because you are the key to unlock this kingdom.

(Three)

Why play these petty games for things you can't change?
Trying to change me and my lifestyle are things you should look past
Because all you will do is come to a complete crash
Ending in a short-lived cessation from things.

You'll receive no blessings
Shaking your head at me, telling me things you want to do
But they don't involve me, just a fantasy of you
And things you would like to be
Things you would like to have
But me speaking the truth makes you mad.

The games our minds play, just to have a feeling
Decay leaving you hollow and empty today
The thought of me walking away
Hurts me more than it hurts you.
It just hurts you because you're losing your armpiece
Finance fleece.

Why not end this on good terms?
The games that are played can be learned
In a new subsection or some new lessons
With someone that will be fit for you.

We can't continue to play these petty games
For things that we can't change
Our best bet is to end this with the same frame of mind
Knowing that you'll be fine.

Finding someone fit for you will be beautiful
And I hope to see it too
So this is my goodbye letter to you
Because I don't want to see you
These petty games you play
I have to ignore.

(Four)

The more that can be said about the things I don't have
You, to start off with
Why it is life doesn't allow me to have you in abundance?
Why can't I wholeheartedly have you for me?
My outflow is nothing but love and affection to you
And your inflow is ignorance and passiveness to me
I feel as if your heart has withheld all I can ask for
But just trying to receive is all I can believe
Now I have been deceived
On what was misconceived for me to believe
The more that can be said about the PERSON I don't have
NEED I SAY MORE?

Look What a Good Woman Can Do With a Good Man *(Five)*

A good woman
The astounding amazement of a man's life
Is always the beauty in his wife
Supportive, constructive, always productive
Beautifully seductive, intellectually destructive
A good woman.

The mind span of these women
Can help a man to build a house, but can also destroy her spouse
Her intellect intersects at the highest interjection of his life.

The phrase is not what a good woman can do for a good man
It's what a stupendously, intelligent, amazing,
beautiful, courageous God
Who *sent* woman
Does to that man!

She inspires him, admires him
She is his all, she is the perfection to a perfectly round ball
She can roll through all terrains of life, as his wife
She's at his side, but yet in front
Leading the way, but she follows him today
He protects, provides, because of the love inside
He puts her first, knowing that she will be with him at his worst.

Look what a good woman can do with a good man!
Expand his life, invigorate a new plight
Illuminate a new light
Starting with kids and ending with years
The growth and exploration are always so nourishing
From her encouraging words
She is a halo to them
Because without her, there is no him.

I Sit Here and Wait *(Six)*

I sit here and wait time begins to go out of date
The phone never rings, I begin to sing
She's gone, she's gone, how is it that our love can
be so strong to have me singing this song?

I sit here and wait time begins to go out of date
It passes me along and I sing a new song
Time is of the essence and she will be my effervescent …

How will I deal with this situation?
Will I spoil my taste just by dealing with anyone
Just to show I am not hung up on your love?
I am above the B.S. I went through, but yet still I love you.

I sit here and wait time begins to go out of date
Why is it that you are late?
Your love, it leaves me in such a state of mind
I can always be fine
But being that it's not there, it's hard for me not to care.

I sit here and wait time begins to go out of date
Days pass along, I am on my fifth new song
Asking myself, where did I go wrong?
Now I realize I can't despise my phone, it was never on
I didn't pay the bill
That's why I am waiting so long
Pay you, bill!

CHAPTER 9

THINGS SHE DO

Words Can't Explain *(One)*

Words can't explain my hurt and my pain
How I'm feeling, in vain
Deep down rooted, I feel as if I've been booted
Kicked to the curb with just a few words
Words can't explain how bad I feel.
This is how I know it's real.

I sit back and have something strong to drink
Some paper and ink, with a lot of time to think
Now let me try and tell you how the two link.

The one brings you down, the other makes the feelings come out
And the paper helps me to spell them out
These feelings that I am feeling
Let me know that the feelings are not healing
So now I am just keeping it real, then.

Life expectancies
Are not expected to be all of me
Unless they are a part of me with thee
Only one I could want in life
I am just drowning in my pain
It shows the same
That words can't explain.

(Two)

Never seen so much glamor without glare
Never had so much prettiness so close that I should fear
Shining from the light
Your skin looks so bright
How can I get your picture home with me tonight?

Hold it within my arms
Hugging you so strong, knowing that I can't go wrong
Just have to find that perfect song
Never knew life can be so cold
But I always knew my days are getting old
Even as life tries to pass me by
I had to stop and just say, "Hi"
To a pretty female who caught my eye
I always knew my eyes wouldn't lie.

(Three)

All I could ever need and desire, you take me higher
With getting me higher, you intoxicate me
Uplift me mentally and spiritually
The way you educate makes me hyperventilate
Gasping for air, however you don't care
You flood me with knowledge, of which I oblige quick
Soak it up sick and use it to my benefit
You nourish my thoughts to help reform
That which I went through (bad teachings)
You correct a path to assure that we last
And stand the test of time
Even if you are not meant to be mine
The life that we hold can sometimes be cold
Just like these past few days
However, by the grace of God we will be saved
And withstand the frigid days to move forward to our next stage
A plateau in life, you as my wife
(My mind is wondering how to get back to being honest again)
A plateau in life
A level we both will attain that will be the same
I pledge to help you as my friend
(To either get your general contracting company
or real estate investment off the ground)
To see you through your goals to the end.

Yours Undeviatingly,
S.G.R.

(Four)

I had to stop and mention
Your beauty
You have me in detention
Cheeks are something worth pinching and kissing
Every time that I mention those lips, they are succulent to a 'T'
I just hope that I can suck on them.

I would pray to see you today
So I can try and take your heart away
If there is a man in the picture, I will give him his bags
Tell him I may have to prevent him
From getting in your heart
Because I fell in love with you from the start
Just by the looking at your picture
I would hope that I could make you more than just my sister
To my soul.

How She Looks at Me! *(Five)*

I knew you weren't the person for me
Hurtfully, you hurt me, it unearthed me
The pain brought me to my knees
But the Earth wasn't there to receive me
You spoke things clear, but I still didn't hear
I wanted what I needed at all costs
And received it.

The sex was so goooood … I was entirely misunderstood
I was dickmatized by your surprise
And you didn't even kiss between my thighs
I was taken aback, I still couldn't relax
I still wanted to ride your lap.

Those different strokes had me thinking there can't be other folks …
Because, because—I am dickmatized!
Mesmerized by your size and the look in your eyes
How could I not realize
That you weren't the person for me?

You even told me truthfully that you got issues you need help with
I let it walk out the other ear, then I throw a fit
I am so dickmatized
That I despise the truth
And think that it's a lie.

Why am I doing this to myself?
This man constantly tells me he needs help
Is he like the rest?
Great sex, daddy issues, mommy issues
Issues with the world, that's why he don't have a girl
Afraid to commit because of the things that he is dealing with.

I know I shouldn't take a man with a burden on his shoulders
But I am getting older
My thoughts are on my ovaries ...
Who knows if they're soon to be over?
So I am ready to settle down
Because these late nights, I do need a hot sex take down
So I ask my friend and she tells me I'm hypnotized
And dickmatized.

Things we women don't realize
Even when we open our eyes and ears
We just seem not to care
So how do I break this?

What She Likes Me to Do *(Six)*

Today's topic of conversation is sex
The sexual pleasures of which your girth measures
Stretching my walls while banging your balls
is fun for us all until your cum falls
Out of you and into me, the flow is so heavenly
Steady streams with orgasmic dreams is all that
is seems without having to dream
My uterus is for you to touch and it's done so effortlessly
That is why it is so pleasing to me
Did I lose you yet on the other side of the phone?
While I think, and I moan … it feels so good to be grown
The noises we make while the bed shakes

My head is banging while our sex music is playing
(sounds like beating eggs with a fork!)
Constant slaps (putting a paper in a fan) then a hand slap (snap)
Then his voice—where is it at?
Where is that orgasm at? You came for me?
But I need more
Now it's time to get more in this pussy for him to explore
He gets up and turns me around
Pushes me down, throw my legs in the air
Then then he sucks on my clit (sound like a long slurp of a lollipop)
But he doesn't stop, now he starts to lick
And it sounds like this …
Licking an ice on a hot day, trying not to let the juices run away
While he talks
He stops and moans, a soft settled hum
It's almost ready to send me home (O)
He starts to suck again
I scream, "I hate you," again, so now that he knows
What's next? He licks in circles and does it at his best
Now all of a sudden, I go quiet … because my pussy is about to riot
I toss and turn, now he gets his turn
He holds me down and starts sucking again
(It's about to go down)
I bite my lip and it ends like this
hummmmmmmmmmmmmmmm
Then licking of an ice along with long
slurpssssssssssssssssssssssssssss
And to make it worse
I came first.

What Her Thoughts Are *(Seven)*

Just a thought for the day
My thoughts for the day
I thought about you today while I was at work
I felt a breeze that brought me to my knees
It reminded me of something you would do
Ice cubes, hot rooms, cool breeze got me feeling at ease
Just the thought of what you would do
Got me thinking of you.

My thoughts of what I need you to do
Tongue kissing, a lot of licking and back shot position
Hair pulling, what I am missing?
You, in this position
You, peeking through the curtains
While I walk in the front door
You coming to me from behind, knowing what's on my mind
Then you take off my clothes
As soon as I enter, you get on your knees and taste this center
I push you back, you say 'relax'
Then you attack
You eat and put me on your shoulders
I say, "I am not young anymore I am getting older"
Then you flick your tongue
By that time I am back to being sprung
Then you bring with the ice because you know what I like
Sucking and swirling, humming, you're my favorite girl again.

Hallway temperature rising, you can see it in my eyes again
A burst … you always make sure I cum first
Then you place me back down and turn me around.

Push me over to six-thirty,
Ass in the air, feeling dirty
Touch my toes, anything goes
First you kiss it, then you hit it
Slowly insert, then draw back for your shot
I am already ready to say 'blood clot'
You shoot, you score, pulling my hair some more
Now I am ready to even the score
After this nap, because my pussy is sore from what you just explored.

My thoughts for the day is
(Knock, knock, knock)
Anyone home?
(Blank stare while at work).

Every Wonder in This World to Me *(Eight)*

Every wonder in this world to me
That's what you are to me
You bring me joy, happiness, peace and self-awareness
You're attentive to all my aspects
You understand my downfalls
Yet you up lift me, raise me to a higher elevation
Than you have ever yet put any man on
You bring up my misunderstandings
You explore realms of the Earth no one else dares explore with me
We tackle, break down walls, that are within our way … of uprising.

You are the lady in my life
You keep me grounded when my head gets too big for my shoulders
You turn over any leaf that has yet to be unturned
To find the answer to the questions
That's why you are every wonder in the world to me
Hopefully I will love you more each day as we grow old
You are every wonder in this world to me.

Not too many blessing came my way until I met you
Since then, I have been blessed to see life in a different way
Soon I will call you my wife
If there is anything I can do to make you happy, I will
Hopefully a child will make you realize
How much I love you, and show you…
You are ever wonder in this world to me.

Yours Undeviatingly,
To My Wife to Be

(Nine)

Damn!!
I am lost for words
How you look to me in this picture; pretty face, tiny waist
Damn, I would love to be in your face,
Talking, kissing, then reminiscing on our first kiss.

You got me thinking about how I would like to be madly in love
Grasping you like a dove
Damn, here I go again—lost for words.
You know, your beauty stands at the curb
Stops traffic without words
They have some saying, you know you heard
Wishing, kissing, here I go again, stuck in a premonition.

Let me not press my luck
Hopefully you understand what's up
And give me a few minutes to just say
What's (pause) what's (pause) whassup?

Her Getting High Off of Me *(Ten)*

My addiction leads me to a physician (him)
Who talks to me in encryption (sweet nothings)
About my street legal prescriptions (sex)
All of these addictions have a different subscription
Some make the heart go flatline
Others thers make the heart race at prime time
Some appease the mind
Others just tingle the spine and make me weak in the knees
Still giving me that high that I need to receive
These highs get me high at the thought of them
Soaring though the skies
Smiling at you entering my mind, body and soul
I need to inhale you or take you intravenously
You don't know what you do to me.

My addiction
This mahogany skin, loving friend/companion
He won't abandon me at my worst
Healing all my hurts
Doctor, doctor, I got this pain from a strain that I inhaled
I need you to give me a remedy
Something encrypted, maybe even prescribed
Your Mandingo / I mean Maryjane
That I pulled is driving me insane
Sucking and touching, kissing and fucking
You are the right physician for some things
Now tell me an encryption that has your prescription.

Endless Affection Without an Erection *(Eleven)*

Can you be my all of which I need?
Can you be my blessing to be received?
Can I look forward to a long life alongside you as my wife?
When I see you, sometimes I become speechless
Because your beauty has me like this.

Your skin is radiant from the sun's beating
Dark brown love, that's your complexion, meaning …
There are many things I need to say
As time comes I will say it.

My speechlessness has me verbally impaired
So I write it down so I can get the words out there
Hopefully you understand my meaning
This endless affection without an erection
Has me perplexed again.

Thinking about being next
To those beautiful, succulent breasts
Thighs, lips … all that I want to kiss
Just pleasing you is what I want to miss.

Clouded Vision *(Twelve)*

Blank stares at my fears, knowing you won't be here
Wishful thinking leads to my drinking, my own personal disintegration
Within a short period of time, this criminal mind
Tries to steal the divine infinity of your heart
Or lack thereof, because I just can't grasp the thought of your love.

My confidence is overbearing
Yours is not caring to avoid the feeling of exposure
Evading the fact that the height difference is what I lack
My confidence is overbearing toward your simple rules to life
I want three 'B's (brains, beauty, booty)
You want two MEs … or just twice my height
For you that would be nice.

I am built to be who I am, short to your defiance
But those who know me are appreciative of my reliance
Those who use my confidence as a stepping stool
To help get them through their moods
I don't consider them to be rude, I consider them to be a tool.

We are all moving machines
That sometimes need tune-ups, oiling or a full overhaul
If the time was spent, you would see how I best suit your needs
Even if my height means you can't perceive
How it can be what you want it to be.

Allow my mechanical skills to thrill
Feel and please you at will
With first getting you out of this clouded vision
And helping you to see my vision
Just allow me the time, so that you can listen.

As Soon as I Walk In, the Things You Do for Me *(Thirteen)*

As soon as I walk in, you walk over to me and give me a kiss on the lips
You let down your hair, shake it out like one of those commercials
So tantalizing and seductive.

You lead the way to the bedroom
Where you have a bath ready and waiting for me
After my long, hard day at work, you help me take off my clothes
As I strip down to my bare body you walk me to the tub.

You kneel as I get in, roll back your sleeves
Reach for the loofah and lather it up to wash my back
And then my neck—all the places that are hard for me to reach
After washing me up, you dry me off and lotion me down
You have some underwear ready for me to wear.

Afterwards we sit and eat dinner that you prepared for us
A beautiful oven roast and some rice and greens, my favorite
We get done eating, we clean the dishes together
And work our way to the bed

We get in bed, we kiss and then
Turn the lights down once again
And under the covers we cuddle
Only to fall asleep on one another.

The things you do as soon as I walk in.

Respond If I Have Sex *(Fourteen)*

Booooy …
What makes you think you're tingling my spine?
You think just a few lines is gonna get me all the time?
I can't doubt the fact that in some areas you don't lack
But I will give you flack
You are able to speak eloquent
Your sex is hell-bent
But your love is nonexistent
So I do feel that in some kind of way
There is something wrong with you
Your heart isn't true
You're not in love.

With you, you're able to please a woman's needs
But not ready to give and receive
Your mental and physical is on point
But a lady of my kind, your heart is what I want
So until you are able and willing to give me all
Your title to me will always be small.

Decent dick, decent mind tricks
And I can contain my emotions enough to continue to do this
So, for your sex that you give, I will always feel some kind of way
And that is because you're not willing to give it all
In all of your loving ways.

(Fifteen)

The hardest thing to do is find you
Life has passed me by, time just seems to fly, I continually ask 'why'?
I have yet to find you.

I looked, I traveled, I have even tried to settle … how she is, is not you
She is not the one I was looking for
She isn't God-fearing, or like-minded
We don't build and destroy together
We just destroy forever.

The feelings we have aren't feelings
They are anguish, aggression, which leads to regression
And me side-stepping…
Trying to make something work that's not there
Is the reason why I don't care.

The hardest thing to do is find you
One-night stands, and finding you with my friends
Alone in a room, naked
Ah, ah, ah at the thought, but the feeling got me caught
There is no feeling
So I do care again.

I look, I search, I think 'I just need to put the Lord first'
He will align my stars, make me see the light from afar
I shall trust in him and He in me
Because the devil has told me enough lies
That made me despise.

With my faith in the Most High, life will go right on finding you
I won't even have to think twice
So with it being the hardest thing
It will also become the smartest thing
Trust in you, my Heavenly Father
Thank you for helping me find my future
As I come closer to You—and her.

CHAPTER 10

TRYING TO TALK TO

(One)

Step up to my speed and enter the race
The chase of the race is not to be replaced
Or substituted, or even eluded
However it should be used quick for misuses
Of unadulterated love with unconditional hugs
With warming kisses from your illustrious mistress
(You, being all parts—mistress, missus,
best friend and lover to the end)
However, with you being my missus,
Enduring kisses is where my bliss is.

Enter this race where hearts get chased and body parts are replaced
With intelligent, like minds that race to the finish line
Overcoming hurdles and potholes that murder two hearts slow
And break them apart, we just need a place to start.
Let's not let one night set us apart; why don't we let that be our start?

And we enter this race were our minds are chased
And our body parts are replaced
With higher thinking and elevated collaborations
Speed can kill, speed can help you receive and transceive
All the mind, body and soul needs
Love and faith … things that can't be replaced or misplaced.

A preacher once told me:
Have faith, and love will take its place and find its course in life
Just speak it to the air and all that you want will be there.

Her mind is as an intelligent lady that can hold me down
And all aspects of life wither, boardroom meeting or in the hood
Up to no good.

Body—something that is pleasing to the eye
And the feeling can be reciprocated, even when we get old
Maintaining our health, pleasing each other
Secretly in disguise, only the Lord knows why.

Soul-being—in tune with one's Heavenly Father
So that we receive our blessing and nothing less
Then the love and care we give out to Him and our families
That is what we are proud about.

Step up to a time of a lifetime, allow yourself to unwind
At least just this one time.

Hearts

A cup of coffee brought me
A blessing filled with guitar stringing lessons
To explore and expand, without even me being your man.

You came with joyful tears, overcoming our fears
While we both embark on our journey, we continuously learn
These lessons of life stressing
Taking us back to our essence, as if we are adolescents.

Your inspiration is contagious
It grows and spreads to everyone around you
This is why so many people surround you
You are gentle and stern
The lessons you teach are well-learned
The knowledge you have is well-earned
From hood antics to boardroom meeting banter.

Leadership you possess
Always come with the right answers
The portfolio of things you can do is miniscule
Compared to things people see you do
You are an amazement and I thank you
For who you are and what you have done
The things that behold us have just begun
Now let's have a coffee date
Just for fun.

Vision *(Three)*

Like a butterfly on a rose
Instead of being a bee on a flower, I am a butterfly on a rose
Just think, I'm like a butterfly to a rose
Not like a bee to a flower
My fight is more graceful
My love is more tasteful
My elegance is more shape-full
That's why I relate to you.

When I fly, you need not ask why
I soar when I flap, I glide on the wind's back
That's why there's no seatbelt attached
Because my terrain has no map.

I travel the Earth to look for what it's worth
I soar over the seven seas and fly where the heavens be
In search of that rose in every state and continent
To show my love is prominent
Most know I'm not dominant
That's why I started off climbing this big, brown tree
I started off ugly as a caterpillar, now as you can see
I climbed as high I could be
I was cocooned on a branch for a couple of days
Here, now, I'm searching for a rose
And that beautiful pose that only the one in the heavens knows.

I am a butterfly to a rose!
One of life's most beautiful poses
That's why when you see me you should know
That Heaven knows
About the love I have that is enclosed
(Like a butterfly on a rose).

(Four)

It is nice to meet you
Glad I can greet you and your warm presence
And all of your blessings.

Maybe someday I can be blessed to have you
Or someone like you
Even though you're one of a kind.

It seems to pass my mind
How I let you slip by
Sometimes I ask myself
Why, Lord, why, did she pass me by?
What is it that I could have done to keep her, or even really to meet her?

Although I saw you in passing
It feels as if my heart met you while my body was fasting
For love of this beautiful songbird, this caramel songstress.

Words that fly above all of us earthly people, I guess … to her
She has no equal
Maybe someday there will be a sequel
And I will rise to be your prequel.

(Five)

I am a sapiosexual
Along with being attracted to your beauty and your booty
(BBB = brains, beauty, booty)
The Sa-pio-sex-u-al has me like, wow!
Mind-blown, face showing
It's hard for others not to know
Great qualities and characters
Infallible logistics, you are terrific
You're magnificent, indifferent
With a gift, with this life, I say it twice … life … life.

That you bless and compassionately give without fathom
You're all-seeing and all-knowing when it comes to what's happening
Yes, I am a sapiosexual
Your intelligence is the best of you
What can I say to get next to you?

Your greatness is an elatedness that predated these just words
You heard that at a glance, seems so upsurge
The fact that you heard means that the passion is in these words
This sapiosexual just wants to get next to you
So I can pick your brain and go insane
From the things that don't excite the lames.

(Six)

Hey
Just wish that … damn, I'm speechless!
You know that … damn, now I'm lost for words
Okay, let's try this again

You know, sometimes in life you wish that you could gain the strength
To try to talk to someone
Who you feel is the most beautiful person you have ever seen
That's what I'm trying to do
But it is just not coming out the way I want it to
All I can say now is I tried, and I tried, and I can only wait and see if...
Maybe, just maybe, I was successful.

P.S.
I can only hope that I am, so that God can bless me again.
He has already blessed me with a chance to see you once on Earth.

Discussion *(Seven)*

HER:
Hello stranger.

HIM:
Hello there, how are you doing?

HER:
I'm good, and you?

HIM:
I am good. You know, always missing you …
and have a need for you in my life.

HER:
Really now?

HIM:
It was always like that. Just that you got someone
in your life, so I left the thought of us alone.

HER:
Oh, okay.

HIM:
Are you still with him?

HER:
Yes.

HIM:
How is that working out? Are you willing
to spend the night with me yet?
So I can wake up to you for breakfast?

HER:

It sounds nice.
NO.
I'm in a relationship.
Can't do that.

HIM:

I know, just the thought of having you entices me.

HER:

I'm being a good girl.

HIM:

You can be a good girl with a bad boy.

(Eight)

Can my thoughts be about you (me trying to talk to a chick)?
Yes, you!
You are on my mind and you didn't even leave my sight
Mesmerized by your eyes
Looking at you is making me realize that I need to be wise
In how I talk to you
Or even walk to you
I need to take my time so that I can work my way into your mind.

Now that I have your attention,
Allow me a moment to mention
Your beauty and how blessed I feel
To be able to have these few seconds
Which can lead to a lifetime.

Can my thoughts be about you in the morning when I rise?
At night when I close my eyes?
Or when I'm in a daydream...
Do you know what I mean?

CAN everything from here on out never be without ... YOU?
MY every word consists of you.
THOUGHTS of a future are closer than what I saw at first sight, let us think alike.
BEcome a part of me, let's make history and formulate the past so we will last.
ABOUT to say good-bye in order to say 'hi' to you on another day ... it was a pleasure to meet you this way.
YOU will enjoy life with the vision of you being my wife ... now think about that as you go on your way, and by the way—you helped me to have a blessed day.

Can I Be Your Internet Service? *(Nine)*

Can I be your internet service provider?
Can I download my files and memory to your hard drive?
Can I upload your knowledge onto my ram cards?
Can I be the backbone to your hub?
Will you let me be that access to the World Wide Web?

Let your search engine come from my server station
We can search and find infinite knowledge
That has yet to be found by those who don't look
We can hack into places we have no right to be in
But still have control enough not to damage and destroy
That which is not ours.

Let us protect each other from harmful viruses out there
Combine with my internet service
My firewall protection is available to you at all times
But you must remember that all these amenities
Are only available to you through my internet service provider!

So,
CAN I BE YOUR INTERNET SERVICE?
YOURS UNDEVIATINGLY,
STRIKER

(Ten)

A THUG'S PASSION
AND A GENTLEMAN'S DREAM
IS TO HAVE A WOMAN LIKE YOU.

YOU, BEING THE PERFECTION OF LIFE, MY WIFE
ANY AND EVERYTHING I COULD AND WOULD EVER WANT AND NEED.

FROM YOUR SWEET, GENTLE, HONEY COMPLEXION
TO YOUR LONG, SILKY, JET-BLACK HAIR
ASS SO PERFECTLY ROUND IT SEEMS AS IF GOD
IS PLAYING AROUND WITH MY EMOTIONS.

BREASTS ARE PERFECT WITHOUT SAG
MAKES ALL THE SISTERS MAD
SMILE IS SO BRIGHT YOU DON'T EVEN NEED THE MOON AT NIGHT.

IF I HAD TO SUM YOU UP YOUR BODY WOULD BE LIKE!
DAMN
YOUR BREASTS BEING A C-CUP, 36 SIZE
3+6 THAT EQUALS **9**
WAIST BEING A 24
4-2 EQUALS **2**
LEGS BEING A 25
THAT'S 5-2, THAT EQUALS **3**
NOW THAT'S **9-2-3 (=4)**
THAT EQUALS A PERFECT SQUARE.
NOW INSTEAD OF HERE, CAN I BE OVER THERE?

Can I be inside your mind
Where things are divine
And where I just want to spend time?

CHAPTER 11

WITH MUSIC

(One)

The way the music moves the soul
It always seems to be untold
It moves your body because it holds the rhythm
Sometimes it hits you cold
Heart jumping, beats pumping, body's thumping
It's the music doing something.

It's the music that's got you wanting more
Wanting and waiting, not hesitating, body is shaking
The beat goes, your feet—aching
Dancing and twerking, just in your world
Its music that has become your favorite, girl
Your head bopping, body popping, non-stopping
Got the soul spoiled rotten.

The way the music moves the soul
Story can never be fully told
Now here is the beat that never gets old
Boom boom bap cha, boom boom bap cha
Boom boom bap cha, boom, boom, boom.

(Two)

Take a minute to see how you inspire me to think about you.
You can find these songs and listen while you read.

1. Donell Jones - *Have You Seen Her*

Looking for you my whole life
And I found you by way of a gathering at a club on a late night
Tagged in a photo with your beauty and presence
Hoping to see you again in life, but in person
To be blessed with your gracious smile, beautiful eyes
I can only pray to get to know you!

2. Donell Jones - *All About the Sex*

I know what I've done might appear to be rude
Sorry if I was; however, if I ever had a chance
To deal with a women of your stature
You would be a lot more impressed than any person can understand
And that is how to keep and treat you
So I use my primal instinct to get through to better understand you
Being the man that I am, I know and understand
An intelligent lady when I see and converse with one
You are her, that's why I know with you
It will never just be all about the sex.

3. Floe Try - *Sometimes You Make Me Smile*

Just the thought of you from the one time we met
Does something to me, and I can say you really make me smile
You help me to see that beauty and intelligence
Still exist in today's times with these women out here
You help me to see a future that can come to pass
Things that I can only hope and pray for
But it can only start with you … and a smile.

Trey Songz - *Sex Ain't Better Than Love*

I was just playing on Sunday
But wish I had the chance to have you for breakfast later on in life
However, loving someone as beautiful as you
Would be more delightful
Knowing that someone like you would give their all back
And help to grow and build on the lifestyle that I'm trying to live
Wishing for and knowing that you are every man's all
Is enough for any man to change his lifestyle for the better
Just to want to be with you because
Sex ain't better then love.

4. Robin Thick - *Mona Lisa*

Allow me to have the chance, or be blessed with your presence
For a cup of coffee, tea or dinner for three
Me, you, and your father, just so I can thank him
For giving the world such an illuminating person to be around
Even if it's too soon to meet him
Let me thank him for helping to create you
Allow your illumination to shine
So I can learn about you
Spend hours on the phone just so that
On late nights we don't feel alone.

5. Bilal - *Soul Sista*

Never have I had such a change in thoughts about one person
Over the course of a day
Feeling as if you are, or hold, a piece of my soul
One which can break and tame the raging lion in the wild
Constant stares at our photo that was taken
With thoughts of it turning into a portrait
Wondering if the feeling is mutual, praying that it becomes so
Only to know that time will tell if you get on this boat to sail
Seven seas of mystery, and to see what will be, will be
Only if you want it to be, my soul sista.

6. D Angelo - *Brown Sugar*

That which I want in life, that I can't have
I desire to really have you, but for a lifetime
Brown sugar insulin pumps into my veins
And gets me high from beautiful sayings.

Yours truly,
Shazardes

P.S.
Music moves the soul; allow it to warm you when you're cold.

(Three)

Let me come in your ears though your speakers
Speak gentle thoughts, the ones that sneak up
Allow me to be in your mind, to make you unwind
Enter your heart … but with lyrics and beats, knowing where to start
Kiss your back and make you have a slight heart attack
Let me vibrate your mind so that you feel me all the time
I am the words that are repetitively heard
Speaking consistently, with persistency
For thing that are meant to be
Along with how you want them to see your vision
I am spoken into fruition with full recognition about my deliverance
Coming into your ears through these speakers is how
I delivered this.

I am a sound
I'm coming through your speakers so you can hear me
My deliverance is accurate
My words have verbs, so the actions are heard
My singular tone speaks from a megaphone
Along with plural ways, hard-knocking, deep-rattling bass
That shakes the cheeks on your face
Vocal chords here and abroad
I am the sound that contributes to it all.

If I Was Able to Get My Way With You *(Four)*

If I was able to get my way with you, what would I do?
I would treat you like a queen, show you all the wonders of the world
Put you on a pedestal, praise you like the goddess you are
Admire you for your beauty
Feed you with the finest foods
Hand-pick herbs to prepare food for you
Wine you with the finest that man has to offer
And if that's not enough
I will lay down my life for you
Because I want you to bear my children
And that's if, and only if, I was able to get my way with you.

(Five)

Are your headphones on? Listen!
Listen to me
Allow me to cum through your speakers
A beautiful sound from your tweeters
Deep bass from your subwoofers, vibrating your walls
Back tingling in all
Earth-shaking, groundbreaking, lyrical heavens
Music that lightens the soul, uplifts the body
Even when it's old
Sensual high pitches along with glorious mid-switches
Altos and tenors, harmonious sinners
Variations and anxiety has this musical session lively
Music is what we make together
Whether it is with sound or our bodies playing around
Let me cum through your speakers
While you blow sub-woofers and tweeters
Enter your mind with these heavenly divine
Sounds of love
Music the blessing
From up above.

A Man Ain't Supposed to Cry *(Six)*

I was told as a child that a man ain't supposed to cry
And that I should lay down and die!
Crying is showing one's weakness
One's weakness is one's defenselessness
The process of showing your tears is giving up the battle
If you give up the battle, then you lose the war
If you lose the war then what was the use in fighting for?
Just to put yourself on a pedestal
And to make it seem as if you're a bigger man
Than who you are at war with?

A man ain't supposed to cry
When you cry, you lose a lot more
Than just what you were working for
You lose all your accomplishments
Everything you worked for is just as if you didn't
Because you worked for something that you can't get elsewhere
Just like love.

A man ain't supposed to cry about love
Love ain't meant to break you down, beat you up and rip you apart
It's not meant to make you cry
If you love someone and they want to leave you
Whether spiritually or physically
You should learn to let love go and not cry over it
We are all meant to lose things in life
Some lose more and others lose less.

But we all know that a man ain't supposed to cry
It's just as the saying goes:
Don't cry over spilled milk
Even if it is your last.

(Seven)

Whenever you get the time, or the moment of the day
I will take you there
Do you have the time right now?
If so, have a seat and let me take you there!
I'm that perfect picture
I'm what you want in life
I'm all that you need and desire
You see me and all that I am worth
You see the gift and the curse
The good and the bad and all the worst
If you compare me to your last, it will seem
like he crashed and had road rash.

Let me take you there, I don't care about your friends
Or all of those women
You should know me
I don't give a fuck—they can all get lost in their own world
While I focus on you
Is it here, is it now, that time and that moment? Wow!
I think you're starting to like me now
Are you ready for me to take you there?
I guess so!
Because you wouldn't be here
If you didn't want me to take you there.

Let me think, I don't want to get too deep—where shall I start?
I don't want you to think that I just want to get in your heart
Okay, here we go! Ready? Let's take it slow
Listen to some Teddy P. and Al G., just to set the mood
Don't want to seem rude, but take off your shoes
The music, it's going … Teddy is singing, 'close the door'
And Marvin G. is getting warmed up
Because sexual healing got you wanting more.

Isley Brothers between the sheets got you taking it off
'Turn off the lights' got you screaming for all the woman
Who never felt this before
Smokey R. got you singing, cruising once more
Ray C. got you saying 'nighttime is the right time'
Al G. got you saying 'let's get married'
Aretha F. got you wanting to be carried (you make me feel)
Stevie W. got your head in the sky looking for a ribbon
Last but not least, Bobby W. got you thinking
About how a woman's got to have it.

And I'm sure I will give it to you
Now that the time and the moment are well spent
Whenever you get the time again, you know how it should begin.

CHAPTER 12

BOOK ENDING

(One)

One hitter quitter
Words that I say come from inside my heart today
Things that have meaning seem to mean them...
Them being those words you want hear
Something new to you whispers in your ear
When all you think is, "He wants to buy me a drink
Just so that he can play in my paint"
When that is not what he thinks.

He wants a full court press so that he can see you at your best
And at your worst, so you can see who leads first
In this game there is no playing the same
You just came across too many lames
So now no need to cure those heartbreaks anymore
When that old person that was a one hitter quitter
Don't play anymore.

Okay, I Got One—Back Seat Sex *(Two)*

2:16amShazardes
Back seat sex in my black car, what's next? A late-night drive in the park, some place dark, ohhhh where should I start?
2:18amShazardes
How about right after the movies? Sometimes that's the best way to do me.
2:20amShazardes
You riding, our bodies colliding, me deep inside and orgasmic proportion that's how we get off in the back seat of my car. I can't believe we got this far. A kiss here, a lick there, then taking off your underwear. Now get over here.
As you ride on top ... Your titties start to rock. Hot and sweaty in the park we already know it's a late-night start.
2:22am Shameika
Lol.
2:23amShazardes
Or a late-night finish as this back seat we diminish. Knee and ass burns that's how we have learned that late night in the park is the best place for sex to start.
lol;-o
2:25am Shameika
Funny.
2:25amShazardes
O yeah, back seat sex it is the best.
Lol
2:26am Shameika
Your back seat just happens to be the place I like to creep, that's why the sex between us is so discrete.

(Three)

I can only wonder if you think about me.
And what your thoughts would be
How do you think about me, and why me?
Have I somehow sparked an interest in you, like you have in me?
Have I yet to see your real beauty?
I can only acknowledge that which I see
I was shown just from pictures the beauty of you
I feel in my arms is where you belong
The future has yet to behold things untold, and papers unfold
On what we want and where we will be
I will tell you now my future is brighter just thinking about you
You are all I wanted
The success of being a college grad
The success of being my own boss
The success of becoming the head of my department
The success of publishing my book
The success of falling in love, and
The success of starting a family
You are my completion
You are all
I can only wonder if you think about me
Future, here I come …
You are a part of me.

(Four)

I come to believe the key to my success is YOU
My heavenly father, YAHUAH
The success of myself, along with the rest of the sinners on this Earth
We are not perfect, but we are worth it
Worth every hassle, to be blessed to wear
Your tassels and holy garments
And praise you and be honored to be your elite few
I thank you for these kind words
And all that we have heard throughout life
So from here forward, the Bible will be in my life
And it will be kissed by me, and
Thank you for my new life.

CPSIA information can be obtained
at www.ICGtesting.com
Printed in the USA
LVHW082018131220
674086LV00006B/87

9 780228 818212